13 Years in a Wheelchair but GOD

Marquetta Killgore

MW00936106

13 Years in a Wheelchair
...but God

Copyright 2015 Marquetta Killgore

Published by Docs2eBooks

Printed by CreateSpace

Cover Design by Melanie Smith

Unless otherwise noted in the text, the scriptures quoted were taken from *The King James Bible*, *The New King James Bible* or *The Amplified Bible*.

All rights reserved. This book or any portion thereof may not be reproduced or used in any manner whatsoever without the express written permission of the author except for the use of brief quotations in a book review.

Contents

Dedication

I dedicate this book first to Jesus Himself, who took the stripes for my healing and to my husband, Jerry Killgore, who never looked at me through eyes of disappointment those thirteen years when our lives were so completely changed overnight; and to our daughters, LaQuita Massee and Lucretia Franetovich, who had to help Mom instead of Mom helping them.

I also thank my mom, dad, two sisters, and two brothers, who all faithfully prayed for me. And I thank Pastor Mark McIntosh for the Month of Miracles he held at our church, and the healing school he held each afternoon that taught me how to receive my healing. I am so grateful for all the preachers and teachers who taught at this month long revival, and for their healing ministries, especially Pastor Mark and Rick Fern.

Thank you all so very much. No words can ever say "Thank you" enough for the countless prayers you sent up on my behalf. Thank you, Father God, for hearing and answering those prayers.

Acknowledgments

Special thank you goes to:

LaDonna Neel for taking time out of her busy life to edit my book.

Linda Fritch for being my consultant, choosing a better title and leading me to Sharon.

Sharon Threatt for publishing this book, giving me wise direction and for the many hours of work to get it ready to publish.

Introduction

In 2004, after being in a wheelchair for thirteen years, I was instantly healed of a progressive, incurable condition called Reflex Sympathetic Dystrophy (RSD). This is my testimony of how I was healed of this condition and what helped me to receive my healing.

Even though I believed in healing, I had what I call walls that stood between me and my healing. This book is a study of what the Word of God really says about those walls. Once I understood what the Bible truly says about healing, I was healed. Maybe you have some of these same misunderstandings. I attended a healing school for about thirty hours in 2004 which helped me understand the truth. I have never stopped studying healing in the Bible.

My prayer is that what I learned in the healing school and years of study and research will help you receive your healing also.

◀CHAPTER 1▶

THE BAD NEWS

I have to tell you the bad news! If I don't tell you the bad news you won't understand what a miracle God has done in my life. When I was 42 years old I was a wife and mother who worked full time with lots of overtime. I was a born again, Spirit-filled Christian who was a very happy and positive person. I faithfully attended church and took my daughters with me. I was very healthy and rarely had so much as a headache.

But the day came when I was hurt on the job, it was just a little injury, no big deal. It became a constant, annoying throb under my right ankle bone which became more and more annoying and painful. I went to my regular doctor and then to a foot doctor. He said, "Wear this sock," and later, "try this brace, get these shoes, try this, or avoid that..."

As the days and weeks went by, the pain moved to include the top of my foot and before long, I had the same pain under my left ankle. I justified it to myself: "I'm favoring my right foot, so the left is just overworked or strained." Then the pain moved to include the top of my left foot, too, becoming progressively worse and going up my legs. Eventually, the foot doctor sent me to a sports doctor in Oklahoma City at McBride's Bone and Joint Hospital. I thought, "Good, he'll figure this out for me."

The sports doctor thought it might be nerve entrapment in my legs. He scheduled me for leg surgery on both legs called bilateral fasciotomy. The fascia is a thin film—like saran wrap—that is over the muscles in our legs. It tightens when you tippy toe and releases when you put your foot down. The doctor thought they had quit releasing and were causing the nerves to be entrapped. He made four-inch incisions on the outsides of my legs above the ankles. He went under the skin from my ankles on the outside of my shins, up my leg and across just below my knees, and back down the calves of my legs to my ankles to release the fascia.

This surgery was considered a simple outpatient procedure. You wake up, go home and you're all better. However, when I woke up I didn't know there was that much pain in the world. They ended up keeping me overnight. Jerry came back the next morning to pick me up and I hadn't slept at all. I was in too much pain to sleep, but I went home thinking it's just surgery pain and it will be alright.

Since the surgery was on both legs, Jerry had borrowed a wheelchair to use for a few days to help me get around. We thought this was just a little detour in life and that I'd be okay in a few days and then we'd go on with life as we knew it. Little did we know that I would use a wheelchair for the next thirteen years! I think God is merciful by not telling us everything that is ahead of us. We would have been so overwhelmed and thought, "We can't do this." But God is faithful to help us day by day.

When you have surgery the doctor gives you pain pills to help you through the first days, but these light pain pills were of little or no use for the amount of pain I was in. I called him and told him that I was really hurting and he gave me the "It will be okay" speech. So I thought, "Well I'm just being a weenie and I just need to hang in there."

As the days went by, I called him again about the pain and he phoned in eight Tylenol 3s which didn't help at all and then later he called in another eight. I went back for my checkups and follow-ups and "complaint-ups" but he didn't know what to do with me. The six weeks off of work ran out and I was supposed to go back to work. Jerry and I didn't know how in the world I was going to work when I could hardly bear the pain even while sitting. My job required me to go up and down stairs several times a day and I could barely walk on level floors at home.

But duty calls, so I went back to work and stayed all day. I was so miserable and in so much pain. My feet were swollen over my shoes and my legs were so swollen that it stretched my incisions a little. When Jerry saw them he was shocked but he didn't say anything "in case I hadn't noticed," but I had noticed. I never went back to work again. I couldn't.

Jerry and I noticed that sometimes the front of my legs were very shiny like mirrors, but we didn't know why.

The sports doctor sent me to another specialist, Dr. Larry Willis, also at McBride's Bone and Joint. The instant he saw my shiny legs he said, "You have RSD!" All I could think was, "Praise God! He knows what it is. Now we are getting somewhere!" He stepped out of the room for a minute, and Jerry and I were so excited! Finally a diagnosis, that's the first step in getting help.

When he came back in the room, I said, "What were those letters again?" He said, "RSD, Reflex Sympathetic Dystrophy," and he gave me a little pamphlet. We had never heard of RSD. Dr. Willis asked me what kind of pain pills I was taking. I said, "None." He was very upset and said, "You have RSD and no pain pills?" So he wrote me two prescriptions for pain along with a couple of other prescriptions. Boy, was I glad.

When we got to the pharmacy and had those prescriptions filled I was so shocked at how many pain pills there were. Why were there so many? I just needed help for a few days until I could get a grip. We didn't know that you should never have surgery if you have RSD. Surgeries cause the RSD to spread to the trauma areas that the surgeries themselves create. Since I hadn't been diagnosed properly, the sports doctor didn't know that. When I went into surgery I was in stage one and when I came out I was in stage three. That's why the pain was so amplified.

I couldn't stand the sensation of touch. I couldn't even stand a sheet on my legs because it made the pain worse. We did discover that a light touch of a downward stroke on my legs helped calm the nerves and lessen the pain. Many nights Jerry would let me lay my legs across him and he would gently stroke them down for hours to get the pain to lessen so I could go to sleep. Much of the time it would be the wee hours of the morning before I could fall asleep.

One of the things I didn't know until I had RSD is that medical science cannot measure pain. I never thought about that before one way or another. They can put a man on the moon but they can't measure pain. There are some clues that help a doctor have an idea of the pain level like blood pressure and sedimentation rates (shows how much inflammation is in your body). Inflammation means pain evidently, but there is no hard and fast test that says someone can't work because they are experiencing a level 8 or 10 on the pain scale. The pain I was in was higher than a 1 to 10 Scale!

Several months after surgery the insurance company wanted to give me a settlement and then walk away. So, in an attempt to figure out what my future was with RSD and what it would mean physically and financially, I took the little pamphlet that Dr. Willis had given me and wrote to the place that said, "For more information, write here." In two or three weeks I received a packet in the mail and it was not good news. I wrote for even more information, and the more I learned the more overwhelmed I became.

I highly recommend that if you get a bad diagnosis do not get on the internet! It tells you everything that could possibly ever happen. Too much information does not help you keep your faith up. The saying *feed faith and starve doubt* fits really well right here, so just go to the Word, feed on that and let the Lord help you out.

The information we received in the mail stated that there is no cure for RSD and that it is also progressive which means it gets worse as time goes on. RSD does a "mirror image" which means if you have it on the right side of your body it will go to the left side also. That explained why my left foot started hurting after I had it on my right foot and then both legs.

It wasn't that my legs mechanically didn't work; they always worked, it was the pain. The more I walked, the more pain I had. On the days I overdid and was up too much or walked too many steps, it would take days to get the pain level back down to what was normal for me. The wheelchair became more and more a part of my life and eventually we remodeled our home for the handicapped.

Dr. Willis had to increase the pain medication. He had me try this one and that one and each one was stronger than the last. I was taking muscle relaxers, antidepressants, tranquilizers, sleeping pills, and other medication for inflammation. Soon I started losing bone density so I had to take medication for that. Then I had to take medication for my stomach because it couldn't stand all the pills I was having to digest! Eventually, I was taking medication four to six times a day and 360 milligrams of morphine a day and I did this for years, but I was still in pain. I was so defeated when he gave me that first prescription for morphine. I didn't want to take it but you do what you have to do.

The Bible says that Jesus came that we might have life and life more abundantly. Sickness and disease are not an abundant life. The day I had surgery my life was completely changed. I was a very active person. I was never sick. I had an immune system a horse would love, but my happy, healthy, abundant life was completely changed. The bad news is that it didn't change just my life but my family's lives. Jerry was a long distance truck driver and he had to get off the road and come home to take care of me. He took a desk job which he hated, but he didn't have a choice. He had to take me to all the doctor appointments, run the errands, do the grocery shopping and even help me with the housework. He was doing things he never had to do before. My daughters no longer had a mom to help them, they had to help Mom.

I was in the hospital a few times, mostly from complications of the RSD, and on three of those stays, my family was told I might not make it. The insurance company also tormented me by sending me to doctor after doctor trying to prove that I didn't have RSD. Jerry estimates that I saw at least sixteen different doctors. I don't remember how many. It was so hard for me to take the trips to Oklahoma City to see them, and the stress of filling out all the new paperwork about what happened, how it happened, and what doctors had done to try and help me. Even worse was the fact that there was no test they could run that would really show how much pain I was in. I cried a lot and prayed more.

Every one of the insurance companies' own doctors said that I not only had RSD but that I'd have to take medication for the rest of my life. You see, it wasn't just one misinformed doctor in some corner office that said I had RSD, there were many. I was declared permanently and totally disabled by a judge in a court of law.

I had gone down for prayer in our church many times through the years and was prayed for by pastors and elders and visiting evangelists. My sister took my brother and me to a church in Norman one time because she had heard that an evangelist there had a healing ministry. I was prayed for and wasn't healed but my brother was prayed for right after me and he was completely healed of heart trouble. That was the first time I realized that **something was wrong with my spirit.** Something in me was standing in the way of my healing. My sisters took me to a Benny Hinn meeting in Oklahoma City one time, but there were so many wheelchairs I couldn't get close enough for prayer.

I had what I call walls in my mind which stood between me and healing, and I didn't know how to tear them down. I would love to say that I just ran to the Bible when I was faced with spending the rest of my life in a wheelchair and in extreme pain, but that is not what happened. I had become a born again Christian at the age of seven, so you would think I would have done that first. I had no idea that it could run into such a serious condition. And being in so much pain and trying to adjust to all these new limitations which had come so suddenly was part of it. I knew God could heal big things but I had so much baggage in my head. I had so many walls which were based on my lack of knowledge about what the Bible really had to say about grace, the love of God, and about healing.

Then Pastor Mark McIntosh became the pastor of our church. We were having a small class one day and I asked him, "Why is it that some people get healed and others don't?" He said, "Many times they don't know how to receive." Then he said, "One of these days we are going to have a healing school." Now healing I knew, and school I knew, but I had never heard of a healing school. I thought, "Are they going to teach me how to be healed?" Even though I didn't understand it, I knew right then and there that I would be healed because of that healing school.

A few months later Pastor Mark had what he called "The Month of Miracles" at our church in August of 2004. It was a thirty–day revival with an emphasis on healing. There were several preachers and evangelists who came and preached and prayed for the sick every night. In the afternoons for two hours each day they had the healing school. Sometimes the visiting evangelist would teach and sometimes Pastor Mark would teach. It was an intense study of The Word, The Word, and The Word.

I was desperate to be healed! I was getting worse and worse. The healing school was my only hope of a way out. The doctors couldn't fix me, they could only help me deal with the pain through medications. With the progressive part hanging over my head and literally seeing myself getting worse and worse, I was running out of options even though it was hard for me to go and cost me physically to go. Just getting dressed and ready to go to the school caused the pain to be worse than my normal. Being out of my routine of always thinking about every move and trying to keep the pain down, now I had to make myself get dressed to be as presentable as I could and then drive to the church.

Praise the Lord it was only five miles away. My right foot was worse than the left but when you drive you have to stretch your leg out to reach the gas pedal, then press your foot down and hold it in that position all the way. When I got to the church I had to unload the heavy wheelchair myself then wheel myself up the incline which caused my hands and arms to hurt. The insurance company by that time had provided me an electric wheelchair for my home. But they would not give me a lift for the back of my car! So when I drove anywhere I had to use my regular wheelchair. That is one reason I rarely left my home. I knew that I had to go to the healing school.

◀CHAPTER 2▶

WALL #1: IS IT GOD'S WILL TO HEAL?

I love to read Christian books about a lot of things, especially on healing, and I'd like to recommend some for you: *Christ the Healer* by F. F. Bosworth, *Healing the Sick* by T. L. Osborn, and *Health Food* by Kenneth Hagin (it is not about food).

However, one book I read left me very confused. I won't tell you the name of the book but the author said that sometimes God doesn't heal you because He is trying to teach you something. That sent my mind into a tailspin. My Christian background didn't teach grace so I had grown up feeling like I could never please God. And if what this writer wrote was correct that meant God holds grudges. I knew that couldn't be right because **1 John 1:9** says, "If we confess our sins He is faithful and just to forgive us our sins and to cleanse us from all unrighteousness." But even though I knew that scripture it still put up another wall and I already had enough, I did not need one more.

I believed in healing all my life and was even healed a few times along the way, but RSD was too big for me. My only hope was a real miracle of God. It wasn't going to happen by being positive because I was a positive person and it wasn't going to be mind over matter. It was going to take the Word of The Living God over my circumstance.

Because of this very popular book and some well-meaning people, I believed some junk that was not even biblical. The healing school taught me what the Word really says about healing, not what someone said the Bible says or what someone feels like the Word means or even what I thought the Bible says, but what the Bible really says about healing.

The first thing we need to know and have settled in our hearts is the answer to the question: **Is it God's will to heal? Exodus 15:26** says, "I am the Lord who heals you." God revealed Himself in the Hebrew text of this scripture as Jehovah Rapha. This is one of His covenant names (covenant is an agreement between God and man). If it was not God's will to heal, why would God reveal Himself as our healer? The Bible says that His Word is forever established. It says in Revelation that not one jot or one tittle will change. Another simple way to prove this is by the sun. It comes up every morning. This proves again that something God puts in motion stays in motion until He dismisses it.

> **Psalm 119:89** —Forever, O LORD, Your word is settled in heaven.

> **Isaiah 40:8** —The grass withers and the flower fades: but the word of our God shall stand for ever.

When Jesus came for His ministry here on earth He said that He only came to do the will of the Father (**John 5:19**). And if He came to do nothing but God's will, what did He do?

> **Matt 4:23–24**—Jesus went throughout Galilee, teaching in their synagogues, preaching the good news of the kingdom, and healing *every* disease and sickness among the people. News about Him spread all over Syria, and people brought to Him **all** who were ill with various diseases, those suffering severe pain, the demon-possessed, having seizures, and the paralyzed, and He **healed** them (NIV).

Those suffering severe pain, it says, and pain was my problem. I didn't know until I read that scripture in this translation that it said pain. That prompted me to see if it said pain anywhere else and I found it also in **Isaiah 53:4** which says: "He (Jesus) bore our sorrows." The Hebrew translation of sorrow is: anguish, grief or pain. I was so encouraged. My need was in God's Word! His Word is so personal. The Word has to become personal to you! Whatever your need is, you will find that it is covered in the Bible.

I encourage you when reading the four Gospels to circle every place that it says *all* and *every*. This will help you to see clearly that Jesus always healed *all* of them from every sickness and *every* disease.

When Jesus was teaching the disciples how to pray the *Lord's Prayer* which is found in **Matthew 6:9–**

15 and in **Luke 11:2–4** Jesus told them: "When you pray, say, Our Father in heaven, Hallowed be your name. Your kingdom come. Your will be done on earth as it is in heaven."

What is God's will in Heaven? **Revelation 21:4–5** says, "And God will wipe away every tear from their eyes; there shall be no more death, nor sorrow, nor crying. There shall be no more pain, for the former things have passed away." Then He who sat on the throne said, "Behold, I make all things new." Jesus said that He came to give life and life more abundantly. Pain is not abundant life.

The pain was so severe that I wanted to be outside my body, but that meant I had to die. I didn't want to die; I wanted my life back. Jesus took the stripes so I could have my life back by being pain free; so I could fulfill my responsibilities as a wife and mother like I needed and wanted to be.

The Canaanite woman in Matthew 15 is the only time that Jesus seemed hesitant to heal someone but even so He healed her daughter anyway. Her faith moved Jesus.

> **Matt 15:22–28** —And behold, a woman of Canaan came from that region and cried out to Him, saying, "Have mercy on me, O Lord, Son of David! My daughter is severely demon-possessed." But He answered her not a word. And His disciples came and urged Him, saying, "Send her away, for she cries out after us." But He answered and

said, "I was not sent except to the lost sheep of the house of Israel."

Then she came and worshiped Him, saying, "Lord, help me!" But He answered and said, "It is not good to take the children's bread and throw it to the little dogs." And she said, "Yes, Lord, yet even the little dogs eat the crumbs which fall from their masters' table."

Then Jesus answered and said to her, "O woman, great is your faith! Let it be to you as you desire." And her daughter was healed from that very hour.

Christians have rights in the kingdom. In **Matthew 15:26** Jesus told the woman that healing was *the children's bread*. When I was in the healing school I didn't even notice that phrase. Since I have been healed I feel almost driven to study healing. And, *the children's bread* sparked my interest. When I find something that rocks my world or strengthens my confidence in healing I call them nuggets because it is like finding gold.

The internet says that bread is called the *staff of life*. It is the most basic food, even the very poor usually have bread every day. When the Lord heals us He is meeting one of our most basic needs. He wants to meet all our needs.

In verse 27 the woman told Jesus that she knew the truth of Him coming to the Jew first and then she said something so profound. "Yes, Lord, but even the dogs eat the crumbs that fall from the master's table." Wasn't she bold to ask for just a crumb? And isn't it amazing that she knew the power of a crumb? That was the only time in the New Testament where Jesus seemed reluctant to heal. But He healed her daughter anyway. Her faith moved Jesus.

Every other time in the New Testament when anyone came to Jesus for healing, He healed them. I do not read anywhere that He told them *God is trying to teach you something, so I won't heal you*. This woman's story is amazing to me.

Jesus told her that He was only sent to the lost sheep of the house of Israel (Jews) because she was a Canaanite and they were Gentiles. The Gospel was not given to the Gentiles until Acts 10 where Peter tells of the vision where he learned that God is no respecter of people.

> **Galatians 3:26** says in part: —There is neither Jew nor Greek, slave nor free, male nor female, for you are all one in Christ Jesus. And if you are Christ's, then you are Abraham's seed and heirs according to the promise.

> **Romans 1:16** —For I am not ashamed of the gospel of Christ: for it is the power of God unto salvation to everyone that believeth; to the Jew first, and also to the Greek.

The timing was wrong because the Jews were to be first. She was desperate for her daughter's healing, so she did not let 'timing' stand in the way of her faith! Other scriptures about the Jews being first are: Romans 9:24, 10:12-15, 1 Corinthians 12:13, and Colossians 3:11.

In **Luke 13:10–12** there is another story along the same lines which had a nugget for me. Jesus was teaching in the synagogue on the Sabbath.

> Verse 11 says "and behold there was a woman which had a spirit of infirmity eighteen years. She was bowed over and couldn't raise up. When Jesus saw her He called her to Him and said, 'Woman, thou art loosed from your infirmity.' Immediately she was made straight and glorified God."

The rulers of the synagogue challenged Jesus about healing on the Sabbath. Jesus reminded them that each one of them loosed their oxen from the stalls for water on the Sabbath.

And here is the big nugget: Jesus said, "Ought not this daughter of Abraham whom Satan has bound all these eighteen years be loosed from this bond on the Sabbath?" In other words, He is saying that she is a daughter of Abraham and she had rights. Jesus said healing is the children's bread and this daughter of Abraham should be healed.

These two stories are so powerful and I hope they help you have a clearer picture of what we qualify for as Christians. Or put another way **Psalm 103:2–3** says to "forget not all his benefits: who forgives all thy iniquities; who heals all our diseases." An intelligent person when applying for employment looks into the benefits that come with the position. When you are *in Christ* and a child of God there are certain rights or benefits to which we are entitled because of our relationship with the Lord.

◀CHAPTER 3▶

WALL #2: THE FAITH WORD

I knew in the healing school they would use the *faith* word and that concerned me. To me, faith was some big, hairy, exalted thing that only a few could attain. The Greek word for faith means: assurance, belief, and believe. **Romans 12:3** says, "Given to every man is the measure of faith." I felt like my measure was a sliver. Actually it says in Romans that we were given *THE* measure. I don't know what the measure is but this scripture doesn't say *A* measure as in a random different measure to different people. It seems to imply it is the same measure for each of us. Satan will tell you that your little sliver will never measure up to permanent, huge, dreadful pain in your face every day. Your measure, he says, will never be enough for that.

We have to have faith to be saved and I was saved. So, the simple truth was that I had faith because I believed! I have always believed in God and in creation. I believe He rewards those who diligently seek him and is the Savior of whosoever will.

Romans 10:17 says, "Faith comes by hearing, and hearing by the word of God." Notice it says *hearing*, not *heard*. Why? If you don't develop that seed from the Word it will not grow and will remain spindly. We live in a world of instant, take a pill and be better overnight. We have instant-on appliances, food cooked in the microwave in a very few minutes instead of an hour or so. We are so used to the microwave that we actually stand in front of it patting our foot for it to hurry. In Bible days, they built a fire which slowly roasted the meat. Developing faith takes time. I was healed instantly AFTER weeks of study and changing the way I thought.

It is a process to get the Word of God from our natural brain into our spirit and train our spirits to believe what our brain cannot see, smell, hear, touch or taste. This does not happen by just hearing a scripture or teaching one time. We have to override our natural senses, and that takes time.

So how do you override the natural? By feeding your spirit the Word of God so much that the spirit receives what the natural brain cannot understand. By reading, rereading, and hearing the Word preached again and again, and by saying, speaking, decreeing, and believing those things which we cannot see with the natural eye. Believing the things that God says are yours and what He wants you to have are as real in the spirit world as what we see in the natural world.

Satan wants us to believe that we do not have faith. **John 8:44** says Satan was a "murderer from the beginning, and does not stand in the truth, because there is no truth in him. When he speaks a lie, he speaks from his own resources, for he is a liar and the father of it."

Noah believed something he had never seen on the face of the earth because it had never rained. There had never been a flood, but he believed what God said **more** than he believed what he could not see with his natural eye and had never heard of because it had never happened before on earth.

Hebrews 11:7: "By faith Noah, being divinely warned of things not yet seen, moved with godly fear, and prepared an ark for the saving of his household, by which he condemned the world and became heir of the righteousness which is according to faith."

Once I realized that I did have faith, and the Word that I was hearing was making that faith strong, one of the walls that stood between me and receiving my healing came down. I could see more clearly what the Word really says. I did have faith, but I didn't have enough of the Word of God about healing to make that faith strong, or have the confidence to be strong and immovable.

When you know that the Word is talking about your situation, it becomes personal to you, and that is when you become immovable. James talks about the double minded person who is tossed to and fro. But the more Word you have in you, the less you will be tossed to and fro, believing today and not believing tomorrow. You are in a battle. Roll up your sleeves. Establish that single-mindedness, and reject double mindedness. Make up your mind to agree with the counsel of the Word.

> **James 1:6** —Only it must be in faith that he asks with no wavering (no hesitating, no doubting). For the one who wavers (hesitates, doubts) is like the billowing surge out at sea that is blown hither and thither and tossed by the wind.

> **James 1:8** —[For being as he is] a man of two minds (hesitating, dubious, irresolute), [he is] unstable and unreliable and uncertain about everything [he thinks, feels, decides] (*Amplified Bible*).

No matter what problem you are faced with in life, you can find it in the Bible because God has seen to it that every subject is in there. If you don't know how to find what God has to say about it, ask your pastor or someone for help who studies their Bible. When you find two or three scriptures that minister to you about your need, then read them, meditate on them and put your energy into renewing your mind to what God says is the answer.

You may need to ask someone to help you learn how to study the Bible for yourself. Get a concordance so you can look up things by subject in your Bible, or learn how to use the center reference that is provided in some Bibles. That can lead you to other scriptures that relate to your subject. You may even need to purchase a Bible that you can understand. Before I found a Bible version that I could understand, I didn't like to read the Bible. I finally confessed that to the Lord—like He didn't already know that—and He helped me. Now I love the Bible.

I cannot emphasize enough that we are in a Christian *walk*, not a *run*. There are no quick fixes for big problems. All these things take time but we can get there with God's help. **The Bible is how we grow our faith**. Don't listen to the enemy, Satan, who nags at you all the time and tries to make it seem like there is no hope for you. That is a lie! God talks to you through His written word. Know what He is saying to you is so important.

Once you understand how to study the Bible for yourself, you will be amazed how wonderful the Word is. It will open up a whole new world to you of understanding and will give you the tools for a more victorious life. That will position you to help others study the Bible and take charge of their lives. The Holy Spirit will help you to understand and soon you will help others. Sometimes when I am talking to someone about something I have learned through reading or a particular sermon I have heard, statements come out of my mouth that are amazing. The Holy Spirit will connect it to something else that I have learned in the past which allows me to explain it better.

> **John 14:26** —But the Comforter, which is the Holy Ghost, whom the Father will send in my name, He shall teach you all things, and bring all things to your remembrance, whatsoever I have said unto you.

Another way you can strengthen your faith is find (or pray for) a Godly friend that loves the Word. I have two wonderful sisters who love the Word as much as I do. When we get together we have so much fun comparing what one learned or a sermon that the other heard. It really helps having all the input of their revelation; it strengthens our faith.

I have a wonderful friend who loves the Word also. This friend, LaDonna Neel, is one of the reasons you are reading this book. She is much younger than I but that has never been a problem. She is the one who talked me into getting a computer. I had never had a desire for one because I didn't know what I was missing without one. She said she would help me learn to use it, and, trust me, she has the patience of Job! I could have never written this book out by hand and kept up with it unless I had learned how to use this computer.

LaDonna had no idea that the Lord was leading me to write a book. The computer has proved to be an invaluable help. Best of all she is a strong sister in the Lord and we talk Bible all the time to each other and encourage one another with the Word. I don't know everything and I never will, but having a godly friend and wonderful sisters is a huge help.

It is important to use what is available to us in this wonderful time we live in. We have a wonderful tool that our Christian forefathers did not have. I want to encourage you to watch Christian television, radios, CDs, and DVDs. They are all valuable tools that will help grow you up in the

Lord. In the U.S. we have Christian television coming over the airwaves 24 hours a day and 7 days a week. Try to make some time in your busy schedule to tune them in when you can. You can listen as you do things that have to be done in the house, or listen to Christian radio stations while you drive.

I recommend several ministers who are easy to listen to: Joyce Meyers, Joel Osteen, Joseph Prince, and Andrew Wommack and there are many more. These men and women have been living for the Lord for many years. Satan tries to make us believe that we have it worse than anyone and that nobody understands. As you hear their testimonies of the things God has brought them through it will give you hope. We absolutely need hope. Through the power of communication that we have today, you can download their stories about what they have gone through and what scriptures in the Bible helped them through.

There is also power in the prayer of agreement; don't go it alone. It is good to have people you can go to for prayer for yourself or family or whatever situation you are going through. It turns the power of prayer up on high. Make sure they understand what you are praying for so they can pray the same way or they may explain a better way to pray. Then when you do pray, you can clearly pray the same things at the same time or what the Bible calls being in agreement.

James 5:14 —Is any sick among you? Let him call for the elders of the church; and let them pray over him, anointing him with oil in the name of the Lord.

James 5:15 —And the prayer of faith shall save the sick, and the Lord shall raise him up; and if he have committed sins, they shall be forgiven him.

Matthew 18:19 —Again I say unto you, that if two of you shall agree on earth as touching anything that they shall ask, it shall be done for them of my Father which is in heaven.

As people see your sincerity in serving and loving God don't be surprised if they ask you to pray about something. I live a fast-paced life and like everyone else I have learned to pray for their request right then under my breath or to myself so I don't forget to pray. Then when I get in the car or somewhere alone I can pray more fully about the need. The Holy Spirit helps me to know how to pray or what else to pray for.

For example, a friend of ours had a serious but delicate surgery. While I was praying for a quick recovery and healing for his body, I realized it would be a good idea to pray against pneumonia. I believe the Holy Spirit encouraged me to pray that. He didn't need to be coughing hard after his surgery. I often keep a prayer list on my refrigerator so I won't forget to continue to pray for them. When people ask for prayer they trust you and know that you will really pray. Try not to be slack in this area, it grows your faith to stand in prayer for others.

◀CHAPTER 4▶

WALL #3: NOT GOOD ENOUGH TO BE HEALED

My church background was a performance-based religion. Because I couldn't do everything right every day, I didn't feel that I was good enough or that I qualified for healing. That is a lie. Just as it is with salvation, it is not about us. It is about Jesus and what He has done for us.

I was a born again Christian but still felt guilt and condemnation. I had been taught that you are saved by grace but then you have to live by the law. My church would have never said it so bluntly, but it had become truth to me nonetheless. Like many other Christians, I felt like I was never good enough and could never really please God.

That wrong teaching had to be overcome by the Word of God. I had to *wipe my hard drive* because it was truly embedded in my spirit. I had to reprogram my spirit with what the Word of God really says. I have always had a heart for the Lord and have studied the Word for many years, but **I was studying the Word through law-colored glasses**. No one can measure up to the Law.

The Lord is so good to me that He sent me some wonderful preachers on the Christian networks that taught me the real truth. I starting watching pastors like Joseph Prince, Creflo Dollar, Andrew Wommack, and the Lord even sent a Sunday school teacher, Lynn Touchette, to my church to teach me grace. I still listen to these pastors on a daily basis to renew my mind to the truth that we are to live by grace (the unmerited, unearned favor of God) not performance.

> **Romans 3:24–26** —[All] are justified and made upright and in right standing with God, freely and gratuitously by His grace (His unmerited favor and mercy), through the redemption which is [provided] in Christ Jesus, whom God put forward [before the eyes of all] as a mercy seat and propitiation by His blood [the cleansing and life-giving sacrifice of atonement and reconciliation, to be received] through faith (*Amplified Bible*).

This scripture rolls the responsibility off us and brings into focus that we are made righteous. We can never get there. We are people and we have flaws. God declared us the righteousness of God in Christ Jesus. He made us righteous. Roll it off because it is not about us. As we walk with God and see how much He loves us, our heart's desire is to be righteous before Him. We don't want to see how much we can get by with but rather trust Him enough to literally lean into His bosom for His help and guidance as we build a relationship with Him and adjust our ways to His ways. Our walk is adjusting and readjusting as we learn His plan. His plan is not grievous; it is a better way.

There are about 7 billion people on the earth right now, and each one has a unique set of finger prints. In fact each one of us has ten different fingerprints! We can each one be identified by our unique DNA, fingerprints, voice prints, and eye retina; even our ears are different from anyone on earth, and there are probably others things as well. Just looking at the 7 billion people all having 10 different finger prints is a lot of unique.

Each one of us has blood vessels in our body that are 60,000 miles long; that's enough to go around the world more than twice. The adult heart beats 115,000 times a day, and by the age of 80 has beat over 3 billion times, and yet we are not plugged into electricity.

Since our God is so exact, and so precise, I cannot believe for one second that Jesus fell short of God's plan in any way, shape or form. He didn't come all this way and leave off the one stripe that would have healed your situation. I believe we can all safely trust that the exact plan was followed down to the letter.

So **being good enough to be healed is not our job**! We can't be that good. God sent Jesus in our place to pay for our sins. We are eternally forgiven. We have been *made* righteous. God Himself is not keeping an account or a list of our sins. He will remember them no more (**Jeremiah 31:34, Hebrews 10:17**). If God is not going to remember them, why should I remember my sins? Our sins are **paid in full**.

If you are a parent, there are times when you may not condone something your child has done, but it doesn't mean that you stop loving your child. Joseph Prince says that parents can help their children understand the love of God by totally forgiving them after an incident has been taken care of and the child understands. He says we should completely forgive and not bring it back up, or remain mad at them. We will all have failures in our lives but we have to find a way in our hearts to move on regardless of our disappointing failures or our children's failures or someone else's failures.

Satan is the accuser, he will remind you of your offenses or of offenses done to you. You cannot stay there. Forgive yourself and others. It is not productive to stay in *if only* or the *shoulda*, *coulda* and *woulda* place. Get over it and go forward. God has already forgiven so we must quit falling for what Satan is bringing up. I just tell Satan, "God has forgiven me, it's under the blood, so take it up with God."

This chapter may seem elementary to some, but for me the weight of past sins was so heavy that they were an obstacle to receiving the healing that Jesus provided for me and wanted me to have. I finally realized that I was worried about a debt I no longer owed because Jesus had already paid it for me. I don't have to pay for what has already been paid. Our job is to believe what God's Word says. We have to accept it as a gift. He wanted the children of Israel to believe that what He said He would do. A preacher said once that the whole Bible could be summed up in two words: Trust Me.

◀CHAPTER 5▶

Wall #4: The Curse of the Law

One wall standing between me and Christ's healing was that I had no idea what I was redeemed from! This is huge news! I cannot write this book without including this chapter; it is pivotal for many Christians.

Deuteronomy 28 lists the blessings for obedience and the curses for disobedience. This chapter helped me understand the goodness of God and how He wants to bless us. This chapter is also directly linked to **Galatians 3:13** which says, "Christ had redeemed us from the curse of the law, having become a curse for us for it is written: cursed is everyone who hangs on a tree." Most Christians know they are redeemed, but I didn't know exactly what I was redeemed from. This knowledge will help us in every area of our lives.

The blessings are wonderful. Don't just skip over these scriptures. Read them over and over and let them become part of you:

> **Deuteronomy 28:1–14** —Now it shall come to pass, if you diligently obey the voice of the Lord your God, to observe

carefully all His commandments which I command you today, that the Lord your God will set you high above all nations of the earth. And all these blessings shall come upon you and overtake you, because you obey the voice of the Lord your God:

Blessed shall you be in the city, and blessed shall you be in the country.

Blessed shall be the fruit of your body, the produce of your ground and the increase of your herds, the increase of your cattle and the offspring of your flocks.

Blessed shall be your basket and your kneading bowl.

Blessed shall you be when you come in, and blessed shall you be when you go out.

The Lord will cause your enemies who rise against you to be defeated before your face; they shall come out against you one way and flee before you seven ways.

The Lord will command the blessing on you in your storehouses and in all to which you set your hand, and He will bless you in the land which the Lord your God is giving you.

The Lord will establish you as a holy people to Himself, just as He has sworn to you, if you keep the commandments of the Lord your God and walk in His ways. Then all peoples of the earth shall see that you are called by the name of the Lord, and they shall be afraid of you.

The Lord will grant you plenty of goods, in the fruit of your body, in the increase of your livestock, and in the produce of your ground, in the land of which the Lord swore to your fathers to give you.

The Lord will open to you His good treasure, the heavens, to give the rain to your land in its season, and to bless all the work of your hand. You shall lend to many nations, but you shall not borrow.

The Lord will make you the head and not the tail; you shall be above only, and not be beneath, if you heed the commandments of the Lord your God, which I command you today, and are careful to observe them.

These blessings are now ours because of Jesus' obedience on the cross. The rest of that same chapter lists the curses that are the result of disobedience. Please bear with me as we look at the curses. However, as we just read, **Galatians 3:13** says we are redeemed (Greek: to ransom, to rescue from loss), so we can turn those curses into positives. For those who are redeemed, these are the things we will never have to endure.

Deuteronomy 28:15 —But it shall come to pass, if you do not hearken unto the voice of the LORD thy God, to observe carefully all His commandments and His statutes which I command you this day; that all these curses shall come upon you and overtake you.

In other words if you don't keep **all** the law to the letter all these bad things will happen to you. This chapter is 68 verses long and the curses are grievous. Please take the time to read them in your Bible. I won't list all of them here but will give the gist of them.

The curses listed in verses 16–64 are the opposite of the blessings, but then the next curses get worse. They promise severe poverty, sickness and disease, worry, confusion, perplexity of mind, being overwhelmed, depressed, and all with no hope in sight. Let's look at a few of those curses in **Deuteronomy 28:65-68**:

Then the Lord will scatter you among all peoples, from one end of the earth to the other, and there you shall serve other gods, which neither you nor your fathers have known—wood and stone.

Among those nations you shall find no rest, nor shall the sole of your foot have a resting place; but there the Lord will give you a trembling heart, failing eyes, and anguish of soul.

Your life shall hang in doubt before you; you shall fear day and night, and have no assurance of life.

In the morning you shall say, "Oh that it were evening!" And at evening you shall say, "Oh, that it were morning!" because of the fear which terrifies your heart, and because of the sight which your eyes see.

And the Lord will take you back to Egypt in ships, by the way of which I said to you, "You shall never see it again." And there you shall be offered for sale to your enemies as male and female slaves, but no one will buy you.

Read this whole chapter sometime so you can see what you don't ever have to go through because the blood of Christ was enough. **Isaiah 53:5** says "He was wounded for our transgressions, He was bruised for our iniquities: the chastisement of our peace was upon Him; and with His stripes we are healed."

It seems to me that depression is almost like a plague among Christians today; but God's Word says we have been redeemed from that and so much more. **John 14:27** reads, "peace I leave with you, my peace I give unto you: not as the world gives, give I unto you. Let not your heart be troubled, neither let it be afraid." This chapter can help us settle forever what Jesus accomplished for us on the cross. **We are redeemed from the curse of the law!** Praise God forever!!

I want to point out **Deuteronomy 28:61**: Also every sickness, and every plague, which is not written in the book of this law,

them will the LORD bring upon thee, until
thou be destroyed.

RSD was not listed there, and maybe that is because it was called something different back then or maybe it is a new disease since that scripture was written. Either way, I can read **Galatians 3:13** to say I am redeemed from RSD. We are redeemed from every sickness and plague, no matter what its name.

Romans 8:2–3 —For the law of the Spirit of life in Christ Jesus hath made me free from the law of sin and death. For what the law could not do in that it was weak through the flesh, God did by sending His own Son in the likeness of sinful flesh, on account of sin, He condemned sin in the flesh. (None of us could live up to the perfect law, so God sent His Son to be perfect for us.)

Acts 13:39 —"And by Him everyone who believes is justified from all things from which you could not be justified by the Law of Moses."

Andrew Wommack explains it like this: the Old Testament is based on our obedience but the New Testament is based on Jesus' obedience. Joseph Prince says that the Old Testament is "do" and the New Testament is "done" (by Jesus).

Program yourself to come into agreement with what the Word of God says about you. I did not know this was in the Bible, but how important it is.

◀CHAPTER 6▶

WALL #5: HEALING IS A FINISHED WORK

Another wall that stood between me and healing was that I did not know that healing is a finished work. I knew that Jesus had taken the stripes on His back for our healing before He died on the cross, but it had not dawned on me that when He said "It is finished" it also meant He had paid the price for my healing. Jesus is not coming back to die again for your kids or their kids or take any more stripes for our healing. He has already done that, once and for all. It is a finished work.

> **Hebrews 10:10** —By that will we have been sanctified through the offering of the body of Jesus Christ once for all.

> It reads like this in the *Amplified Bible*: And in accordance with this will [of God], we have been made holy (consecrated and sanctified) through the offering made once for all of the body of Jesus Christ (the Anointed One).

The price for salvation has already been paid for and I KNEW that part. But Jesus is also not going to take one more stripe for my healing or yours because He has already done that, too, and it is finished!

I knew that I knew that I knew I was born again, but I did **not** know I was already healed. I thought He was **going to** heal me in the future. I didn't know He **had already** healed me back on Calvary's cross. It was a done deal 2,000 years ago. I had believed in healing my whole life so I was ahead of many people who don't believe healing is for today; but I didn't know that healing was mine **now**.

Satan can deceive us in so many ways, like sitting on the church pew for fifty years waiting for God to tell you what to do with your salvation. God told us in Matthew and Mark: "Go into all the world and preach the Gospel to every creature." But Satan will say you don't know enough. But, if you know the Lord, you know more than thousands.

If you are a person who believes in healing, then Satan will try to deceive you into thinking, "Okay, God heals, so He will heal you someday." He wants you to believe in the sweet bye and bye. He definitely doesn't want you to believe for the **here and now**.

Many people believe that healing is a thing of the past, but healing is part of the Atonement of Christ. If salvation is still for today, then healing is for today. He died for our sins and took the stripes on His back for our healing on the same day.

John 17:4 —I have glorified You on the earth. I have finished the work which You have given Me to do.

Jesus came to do the will of the Father. **John 17:4** says He finished the work that God sent Him to do. Part of that will was a healing ministry. Jesus took the stripes right before He died for our sins, this was after His own healing ministry was completed. Jesus did not heal anyone on earth after He rose from the dead, so why did He take those stripes unless it was for our healing, today? If He died for *our* sins that day, then *who* did He take the stripes for on that same day?

Once we realize that the stripes were taken so we could be healed and that those stripes were already done for us 2,000 years ago because Christ was finishing the will of God and was what God sent Him here to do, then we can receive our healing by *faith* (believing), in the finished work of the stripes that Jesus has already taken for us.

We are saved through *faith* by *believing* that Jesus died for our sins. We are healed by *faith* by *believing* that Jesus took the stripes for us. We cannot learn enough of the Word to be saved we can only be saved by accepting the finished work of Jesus who died for us in our place. We cannot be healed by knowing enough of the Word to qualify for healing. Healing has to be received by *faith* that Jesus bore those stripes so we can be healed, that is also by *faith*.

We are in a *faith* walk. We receive everything Christ accomplished for us, by *faith* in the finished work. We study the Word to know what God's will is. That will was paid for when Jesus fulfilled God's will. We receive that finished work by *faith*. It is not because we have read enough of the Word, or said the Word enough times. We do those things to get into our spirit what the finished work of Christ is; but healing is always received by faith in the finished work of Christ.

Isaiah 53:5 says we *are* healed and **1 Peter 2:24** says we *were* healed. The Old Testament looks forward to the cross and the New Testament looks back to the cross.

> **2 Peter 1:3** —For His divine power has bestowed upon us all things that [are requisite and suited] to life and godliness, through the [full, personal] knowledge of Him who called us by and to His own glory and excellence (virtue).

> **2 Peter 1:4** —By means of these He has bestowed on us His precious and exceedingly great promises, so that through them you may escape [by flight] from the moral decay (rottenness and corruption) that is in the world because of covetousness (lust and greed), and become sharers (partakers) of the divine nature.

The Bible is very clear that His death was for the sins and the stripes were for healing. **1 Peter 2:24** says: "who Himself bore our sins in His own body on the tree, that we, having died to sins, might live for righteousness—by whose stripes you were healed." They were two separate things but He paid almost the same price for our healing as He did for our sins. He was beaten worse than any beating.

Isaiah 52:14 talks about the hideous beating Jesus endured for our healing; it says that people were stunned by the appearance of His body being so disfigured, more than any man (or the worse possible beating). **Psalm 22:17** says you could even see His bones.

Everything that Jesus endured on earth was for the purpose of helping us. This beating was not a mere spanking, it was so grievous that He could not even walk and someone else had to carry the cross for Him. When I hear people discount that ordeal as though it didn't even count or make a difference for us, it breaks my heart.

As I previously mentioned, the Lord sent Lynn Touchette, a Sunday School teacher, to our church who taught about grace. At times in her teaching she would say that **salvation is not just missing hell but it is the "whole package."** I studied the word *salvation* in the Greek and Hebrew to see exactly what salvation means to us. I have created the following abbreviated list; it is not an exhaustive list by any means. The words in bold letters come from the definition of salvation. I have included a shortened version of the Greek and Hebrews meanings for each of these words. This should make it very clear what each one means:

Deliverance —Freedom, forgiveness, liberty, remission (This means deliverance from the old lifestyle of going through life without having God as Lord of my life teaching and helping me along the way; and in freedom from addictions).

Help —Surround as in to protect, aid, to loose, fortify, defend, to be open, to be safe.

Safety —Refuge, assurance, confidence, secure, prosper, certainty.

Victory —Deliverance, help, triumph, success, subdue, conquer, overcome, prevail.

Prosperity —Goods in the widest sense, or good things. This word has two meanings: That things will go well for us as we walk with the Lord and that we have enough money for the things we need, to help others financially, and to send the gospel through missionaries or television ministers.

Prosper —To push forward, be profitable, have good success, teach, understand, wisdom, wise, succeed in reaching, and succeed in business affairs.

Health —Cure, deliverance, happy, peace, favor, rest, curative, medicine, rest, sound, wholesome, and to have sound health, to be well.

Save —Recover, repair, restore, preserve alive, quicken, revive, and make whole.

Open —To open wide, loosen, let go free, break forth, burst out, increase, scatter.

Free —Liberty, innocent, spread loose, cleanse, clear, (hold) guiltless, innocent, unpunished, not a slave, free born, unrestrained.

Defend —To be open wide, or free, safe, avenging, deliver, help, preserve, rescue, get victory.

Preserve —To revive, to give (promise life), keep alive, quicken, recover, repair, restore, be whole.

Rescue —Defend, get victory, to turn back, (away), return to the starting point, recall, recover, restore, and etc.

Liberty —To remove rapidly, freedom, broad, large, exempt from bondage or care, pardon, relief, loose, or to go at pleasure, remission, deliverance, forgiveness, unrestrained.

Power —Power of God, force, miraculous power, ability, abundance, meaning, might, or worker of miracles.

Amazing! The word *salvation* means healing, recovery, restoration, repair or being well! I didn't know that being born again promised that I could have healing. It also covers prosperity! When I chose to follow Jesus and make Him Lord and Savior of my life, His salvation qualified me for much more than just escaping hell.

The New Testament says that Jesus was moved with compassion. In **Matthew 14:41**, and **Mark 6:34** He was moved with compassion because the multitudes were as sheep without a shepherd. (He is our shepherd Psalm 23.) He was also moved with compassion in **Matthew 14:14** and **Luke 9:11** for those who had need of healing. In **Matthew 14:15–21** and in **Luke 9:13** He was moved with compassion because they were hungry and He fed them.

Philippians 4:19 says in part: My God shall supply all your needs. I looked up the Greek to see what the word *all* means: Any, every, the whole, (all manner of, all means of), always, anyone, every way, as many as, whatsoever, and whosoever. In thirteen different places in the New Testament, Jesus said *made whole.* I looked each one up for the Greek to see what *whole* means: cure, heal, make whole, healthy, well, (in body), make perfectly whole, sound.

Do you need His salvation? Jesus died for your sins. When you pray and ask Jesus to be your Savior, it is by faith you accept the finished work Jesus did for you. That finished work of salvation includes your healing. You do not have to beg Him for five years to forgive you and be your Savior. Jesus made salvation available for you and you only have to accept His provision and receive salvation.

Do you have need of healing? It was included in the salvation package. You now know that it is God's will for you to be healed, and that Jesus took the stripes for your healing. It is a finished work. Just accept His provision and receive your healing.

◄CHAPTER 7►

WHY THE WORD?

The book of 1 John says *we know* seventeen times. There are some things we can know and not have any reason to doubt. These verses in chapter 5 are among my favorite ones. Let's look at them in the Amplified Bible:

1 John 5:14 —And this is the confidence (the assurance, the privilege of boldness) which we have in Him: [we are sure] that if we ask anything (make any request) according to His will (in agreement with His own plan), He listens to and hears us.

1 John 5:15 —And if (since) we know that He listens to us in whatever we ask, we also know [with settled and absolute knowledge] that we have [granted us as our present possessions] the requests made of Him.

If we don't know what the Word says, we pray vague prayers. To have power in prayer, you must get the Word into you. 1 John says "this is the confidence that we have in Him." We are not regular citizens of the world, if we ask anything that is in agreement with the promises in His Word—and the Word is His will—then we know He listens and we know He grants our request. I love knowing that if He hears us we have the petitions that we ask of Him. Isn't it wonderful? As born again Christians there are some things that we can know, not vaguely, but firmly know!

> **Hosea 4:6** —"My people are destroyed for lack of knowledge." When we read the Word of God, we don't do so for points. Reading and studying the Word teaches us what God wants us to have and what authority has been given to us.

> **Proverbs 4:20–22** —"My son, give attention to my words; incline your ear to my sayings. Do not let them depart from your eyes; keep them in the midst of your heart; for they are life to those who find them, and **health** to all their flesh."

All the promises in the Bible are ours, but if we don't know the promises we can't believe for them. When we know these promises we can understand what God has provided for us and wants for us. Then we ask the Father for these promises and come into agreement with what the Word says we can have. **That is when we see results to prayer**. We don't agree with the Word to beat God up with *you said*, but agree with His will of provision in whatever area we are in lack. Our quest is to find out what the promises are so we can believe for and receive them and teach them to our children so they can have them.

If a rich uncle died and left you money or valuables in his will but you didn't know it, that wouldn't be much help to you. Or, if you knew you were in the will it can't come into effect until the uncle passed away. The Bible is a contract. You are in it and Jesus has died for you, so it has come into effect. You are now—today, this minute—a beneficiary to all the promises and He won't withhold any of them from you. Like the uncle, Jesus laid up provision for you. The Bible is God's will and testament for us believers. We must believe what the Bible says.

Psalm 84:11 —"For the Lord God is a sun and shield; the Lord will give grace and glory; no good thing will He withhold from those who walk uprightly." What a wonderful promise! Before you start thinking I don't qualify because I don't walk uprightly, let me remind you that Jesus made us righteous. We qualify because of His work on the cross, not our works. He is our righteousness. And isn't healing a good thing? He will withhold no good thing it says; or you can read it as He will not withhold healing from those who walk uprightly!

I am a doer, a Martha, with all the good and bad qualities of Martha. But all of a sudden I had become a burden to my family. The Martha in me wanted to be there for my family. I wanted to be the helper instead of the helpee; but my hands were tied. I was the ball and chain around my family's necks and I didn't want that. My young daughter had to go to the grocery store for me. She would come to the car and say, Mama, it costs so much! She should never have had to worry about a budget or doing the shopping for the family. At that time, my husband was a truck driver so we had to fend for ourselves when he was gone.

It wasn't long until my husband had to quit a job he loved and take a job that he hated because I was not getting better but worse. When he was gone, it was me and a ten year old child trying to figure out how to do life. That broke my heart. I wanted out. I couldn't do this to my kid. I was supposed to be the mom, not the baby. I not only had the pain of the RSD, but also the guilt of what the RSD was doing to my life and my husband and my children's lives.

> **Romans 8:31–32** —What then shall we say to these things? If God is for us, who can be against us? He who did not spare His own Son, but delivered Him up for us all, how shall He not with Him also freely give us all things?

He is so for us. He gave the only thing that He only had one thing of. In the Garden of Eden God told Adam and Eve they could freely eat of all but one tree. And as we just read, it says He will withhold no good thing from us. That is His heart. Hear His heart and believe in it.

The Word renews our mind to what is God's will, and tells us His heart and what He wants for us. That will is found in the Word. His will is a good thing. His will is not mean or bad. It is so much bigger than what we know. **Romans 12:2** says "be transformed by the renewing of your mind, that you may prove what is that good and acceptable and perfect will of God."

Jesus used the Word to defeat Satan when He was tempted in the wilderness:

> **Luke 4:1–13** —Then Jesus, being filled with the Holy Spirit, returned from the Jordan and was led by the Spirit into the wilderness, being tempted for forty days by the devil. And in those days He ate nothing, and afterward, when they had ended, He was hungry.
>
> And the devil said to Him, "If You are the Son of God, command this stone to become bread." But Jesus answered him, saying, "It is written, 'Man shall not live by bread alone, but by every word of God.'"
>
> Then the devil, taking Him up on a high mountain, showed Him all the kingdoms of the world in a moment of time. And the devil said to Him, "All this authority I will give You, and their glory; for this has been delivered to me, and I give it to whomever I wish. Therefore, if You will worship before me, all will be Yours."
>
> And Jesus answered and said to him, "Get behind Me, Satan! For it is written, 'You shall worship the Lord your God, and Him only you shall serve.'" Then he brought Him

to Jerusalem, set Him on the pinnacle of the temple, and said to Him, "If You are the Son of God, throw Yourself down from here. For it is written: 'He shall give His angels charge over you, to keep you,' and, 'In their hands they shall bear you up, lest you dash your foot against a stone.'"

And Jesus answered and said to him, "It has been said, 'You shall not tempt the Lord your God.'" Now when the devil had ended every temptation, he departed from Him until an opportune time.

Jesus is our example and He fought the devil with the Word and here Jesus shows us to use the Word as our weapon or bullets to defeat the enemy when he comes against us. No matter how you look at it, we are in a battle. Notice in verses 3 and 9, Satan said, "**IF** thou be the Son of God." Satan was trying to create doubt in Jesus' mind about His Sonship. That's the way Satan tempts us, he wants us to doubt the sonship that we have through salvation. He wants us to doubt the blessings that are ours through Christ.

I want you to also notice that Jesus *spoke* the word to Satan. He didn't *hope* the Word, although hope is good. And He didn't *think* the Word, although that is good too. He *spoke* the Word to resist the devil.

Psalm 119:105 says the Word *is a lamp to my feet and a light to my path.* We don't have to stumble around in the dark, the Word will show us the right way as we study, and believe God for great and mighty things.

Proverbs 2:6-12 —For the Lord gives wisdom; from His **mouth** come knowledge and understanding; He stores up sound wisdom for the upright; He is a shield to those who walk uprightly; He guards the paths of justice, and preserves the way of His saints.

Then you will understand righteousness and justice, equity and every good path. When wisdom enters your heart, and knowledge is pleasant to your soul, discretion will preserve you; understanding will keep you, to deliver you from the way of evil, and from the man who speaks perverse things.

Verse 12 says to deliver us *from the way of evil*. The Hebrew definition of evil here is adversity, affliction, bad, calamity, harm, hurt, misery, sorrow, trouble. If you are experiencing any of these problems, then the understanding, knowledge and wisdom found in the Word will deliver you. When we have this wisdom and knowledge of the Lord tucked away in our hearts, we will become more effective in defeating the fiery darts of the enemy.

We talked about **Proverbs 4:20–22** earlier, but let's look closer at the Hebrew definitions: "My son, attend to my words; incline your ear unto my sayings. Let them not depart from your eyes; keep them in the midst of your heart. For they are life unto those that find them, and health to all their flesh."

If you insert the Hebrew meanings to the words in this scripture, it reads like this:

My son, hear and observe my words, extend or stretch your ear unto my sayings; let them not depart from your eyes, keep them in the middle of your heart. For they are living things alive to those that find or take hold of them, and healing, a medicine and a cure to all their body, and a cure for your body or yourself.

Joseph Prince talks about times when doctors can't do surgery because the problem is too close to a vital organ making the surgery too risky. But, the Word of God is so sharp, so precise and so exact that it can penetrate and heal the exact spot without harming the vital organ.

Hebrews 4:12 —For the word of God is living and powerful, and sharper than any two-edged sword, piercing even to the division of soul and spirit, and of joints and marrow, and is a discerner of the thoughts and intents of the heart.

Isaiah 55:9–11 —"For as the heavens are higher than the earth, so are My ways higher than your ways, and My thoughts than your thoughts. For as the rain comes down, and the snow from heaven, and do not return there, but water the earth, and make it bring forth and bud, that it may give seed to the sower and bread to the eater, so shall My word be that goes forth from My mouth; it shall not return to Me void, but it shall accomplish what I please, and it shall prosper in the thing for which I sent it."

This is an amazing verse. Let's look at the Hebrew definitions of these words. *Return*: turn back; *void*: ineffectually, empty, in vain; *accomplish*: do or make, bring forth, bring (come) to pass; *please*: desire, have pleasure; and *prosper*: push forward, cause to, effect, or make to. So this verse can be read like this:

So My Word which goes forth out of My mouth shall not turn back ineffective or empty, but will bring to pass that which I desire or have pleasure in, and it will cause to or effect what I send it to do.

How does His Word turn back to Him? When we stand on the Word and speak the Word it will bring to pass the promises of God and His Word will be effective in bringing to pass the things that God is pleased for us to have. **Matthew 24:35** says, "Heaven and earth shall pass away, but My words shall not pass away."

Numbers 23:19 —"God is not a man that He should lie; nor a son of man that He should repent. Has He said, and will He not do? Or has He spoken, and will He not make it good?" Here are the Hebrew meanings for *lie*: deceive; and *make it good*: confirm. He will not deceive us and will always confirm His word (see also Hebrews 6:18).

Isaiah 14:24 —The LORD who rules over all has taken an oath. He has said, "You can be sure that what I have planned will happen. What I have decided will take place" (*New International Reader Version*).

◀CHAPTER 8▶

THE POWER OF THE SPOKEN WORD

The following scriptures show us that there is power in speaking the Word of God over our circumstances.

> **Proverbs 18:21** —Death and life are in the power of the tongue: and they that love it shall eat the fruit thereof.

We have choices. The power of our tongues makes that choice and sets it in rock. What you say sets the things you say in motion and into being. The doctors had said things over me but I had the power to wipe that out, dispossess it or have power over it. I could agree with the doctor's report, or I could agree with what the Word says. And I chose to believe what God said. I chose life. In a wheelchair and in terrible pain and a problem to your family is not life; so I chose life.

> **Deuteronomy 30:19** —I call (I testify, charge earnestly, give warning) heaven and earth as witnesses against you, that I have set before you life and death, blessing and cursing: therefore choose life that both you and your seed may live.

In the *New Living Testament* (NLT) this scripture reads: "Today I have given you the choice between life and death, between blessings and curses. Now I call on heaven and earth to witness the choice you make. Oh, that you would choose life, so that you and your descendants might live!"

Did you know that we have choices about life and death? When we make choices it not only affects us but others. You choose life by connecting with what the Word says and speaking it over your circumstances, out loud; not just thinking it, but speaking it.

Mark 11:22-24 —So Jesus answered and said to them, "Have faith in God. For assuredly, I say to you, whoever **says** to this mountain, 'Be removed and be cast into the sea,' and does not doubt in his heart, but believes that those things he **says** will be done, he will have whatever he **says**. Therefore I say to you, whatever things you ask when you 1) **pray**, 2) **believe** that you 3) **receive** them, and you will 4) **have** them."

Jessie Duplantis says that we were never called to be mountain climbers but to be mountain movers. What is the mountain in your life? Speak to it and tell it to be removed and cast into the sea. Be tenacious, don't give up in well doing. Keep speaking to the mountain with the Word of God until you see results.

You see, hear, touch and taste your current situation. Satan will not give up easily. It is a fight. Keep saying it, keep believing God's Word, keep searching the Word and saying it until all parts of your being believe what your mouth is saying; or until you know that you know. At first you may find it difficult to believe. But your spirit does believe. Feed your spirit and determine that your mind and spirit together will agree with God.

God has established His promises, and when we find the scripture that applies to our specific need, we have to read that promise, say it, and download them into our spirit until what we see, feel or think is overruled and we can make that connection. Determine to connect with what God wants you to have.

The Word, spoken out of your mouth, meditated on and stored in your heart gives you victory over sickness, disease, and the problems of this world. Notice how many times the following scriptures say **word**, **mouth**, and **meditate**:

> **Joshua 1:8** —This book of the law shall not depart from your **mouth**; but you shall **meditate** in it day and night, that you may observe to do according to all that is written in it. For then you will make your way prosperous, and then you will have good success.

Moses had passed away and God was telling Joshua to lead the Children of Israel into the Promised Land. He gave him this scripture of how to lead this great people. The Lord told Joshua this is the way you can do it with great success. This same principle will help us have great success in this world.

> **Isaiah 59:21** —As for me, says the Lord, this is My covenant with them: My Spirit who is upon you, and **My words** which I have put in your mouth, shall not depart from your **mouth**, nor from the **mouth** of your descendants, nor from your descendants' descendants, says the Lord, from this time and forevermore.

Teach the word of God to your children and grandchildren so that the Word with all its power can come out of their mouths also. The Word is our weapon against Satan, and against sickness and disease when we declare all that the Atonement has provided for us.

> **Job 22:28** says, —"You will also **decree** a thing, and it will be established for you." The Hebrew meanings are: *Decree* means decide; a *thing* is a promise (it has to line up with a promise that the Lord has given us in His Word) and *established* means it will succeed.

> The *Amplified Version* says it like this: "You shall also decide and decree a thing, and it shall be established for you; and the light [of God's favor] shall shine upon your ways."

Be careful with the words that come out of your mouth. **Proverbs 6:2** —"You are snared with the **words** of your **mouth**; you are taken with the **words** of your **mouth**." If you *speak* defeat, worry, and being overwhelmed then you *will be* defeated, worried and overwhelmed. Your own words can ensnare you and set you up for defeat. When you speak God's promises over your life, you will have victory in your life.

We all know people who are what we would call a "Negative Nelly." They are always negative, complaining about everything. They never seem to have hope, they say things like "I can't," "I won't ever," and "I never." They are not pleasant to be around. When the Word tells us to watch the words we say, it is not for harassment but to show us a better way.

Growing up, our family was poor as far as the standards of some families around us, but we were never deprived of food. My dad didn't know that words were important. He called our home the poor farm. He would say, "Come over to see us so you can see how poor folks live." If you talk poverty you may be setting yourself up for lack in your life. We serve a God of abundance who promised He would meet all our needs. And He is not a liar.

After Jesus told the parable of the sower found in **Mark 4:3**, the disciples asked Him to explain the meaning. In Verse 14, He said the *Word is the seed*. You are planting seed when you speak the Word of God. If you plant tomatoes you do not get corn, so what are your words planting? In verse 15 it tells us that Satan comes immediately to steal the Word. Why does he come immediately? He does not want the Word (seed) to take root. Reading the promises, speaking them and hearing them over and over produces faith and calls those things that are not as though they were.

We are created in God's image and He spoke the World into existence. There is power in our tongue. In *The Power of Speaking God's Word*, Creflo Dollar brings out something I had never noticed. In **Genesis 1** when God said "Light be" He didn't say anything about the darkness. He didn't address it at all! He just spoke what He wanted, which was light.

> **Psalm 19:14** —Let the **words** of my **mouth**, and the **meditation** of my heart, be acceptable in Your sight, O LORD, my strength, and my redeemer.

> **Joel 3:10** —Let the weak (Hebrew: frail) **say** I am strong.

> **Psalm 107:2** —Let the redeemed of the LORD **say** so.

We can start by saying the Word of God over ourselves and our children. We must speak the Word over our situation, no matter what bad words the doctors say or what the circumstance looks like.

> **Galatians 6:9** —And let us not be weary in well doing: for in due season we shall reap, if we faint not.

Never, ever give up, continue to speak the Word over your problems, concerns and sicknesses.

◀CHAPTER 9▶

The Power of Your Thoughts

Deuteronomy 7:18: —If you should say in your heart, "These nations are greater than I; how can I dispossess them?"—you shall not be afraid of them, but you shall remember well what the Lord your God did to Pharaoh and to all Egypt.

Our thoughts have power. In this scripture the Lord told them what **not** to think in their hearts. They were thinking in their hearts: They are too big for us, how can we dispossess them? But He told them what to say. He corrected their thinking. Just like we have to change or correct our thinking and what we say. God told them to do this! And then He told them to remember what He had done to Pharaoh and to all Egypt. In other words, like David says often in the Psalms, encourage yourself in the Lord. Remember what He has done for you in the past and think on those things!

The question I have for you is this: **What are you saying in your heart?** If you are thinking this is too big, too hard, then God's hands are tied. He cannot do what He needs to do in your life. When thoughts came to my mind such as no cure, progressive, and declared by a judge in a court of law permanently totally disabled, I had to renew my mind to what God said in His Word rather than what the doctors and the judge had to say. That means I *deliberately* changed my thoughts and words to agree with what God said. The Word of the Living God is the final word; it has more authority than man. Of course Satan doesn't want you to know this. If he can keep a war going in your mind he is a happy camper.

Also, remember that the Children of Israel sent twelve spies to the Promised Land to spy it out. Ten of those spies came back with what the Word calls an evil report. It was called an evil report because they didn't agree with what God had told them. They said in **Numbers 13:33** *we are as grasshoppers in our own sight.* They were not grasshoppers in God's sight, because God had promised them the land.

Caleb and Joshua said we are well able to possess it and they were the only two of that generation who did go in and possess it. At the age of eighty Joshua said, "Give me this mountain." God went before him and he won some of the greatest battles in the Bible. God is looking for people who will believe what He has said.

I just want to remind you of the obvious: The Most High God spoke the world into existence, He hung the stars in the sky and He calls them by name. He led the Children of Israel through the wilderness, probably two and a half million people, He fed them and their herds and flocks every bite of food and every drop of water for forty years.

> **1 Kings 8:56** — "Blessed be the LORD, who has given rest to His people Israel, according to all that He promised. There has not failed **one word** of all His good promise, which He promised by the hand of Moses His servant." He is the same God now, as He was then.

These miracles were done for people who were living under the law and missing it every day. They murmured continually, but God still kept His promise **down to every word**; not because of *their* goodness but because of *His* goodness. We don't live under the law but under grace, which is a new and better covenant. Praise God the new covenant is certainly not about how good we are but about what Jesus did for us in the atonement.

So, the Bible tells us what to think on and what not to think on. Please don't be discouraged about this, rather be encouraged. **The Bible is our 'How-To Book.'** The acronym for BIBLE is said to be *Biblical Instruction Before Leaving Earth*. God is practical and wants to teach us a "better way" through His Word because He loves us.

God has thoughts about you. There are many scriptures that tell us what His thoughts are. They are good and wonderful. Probably the most well-known is **Jeremiah 29:11**: —"For I know the thoughts that I think toward you, says the LORD, thoughts of peace and not of evil, to give you a future and a hope." **Psalm 40:5** is another good one. Search them out and meditate on them and teach your heart to trust in His goodness and kind thoughts toward you.

So, what are you thinking? Are you thinking what God says about you or are you thinking what the world says? Or, are you thinking about what you "feel" about yourself? Or, are you thinking about past failures? God has already forgiven you for those and He is not thinking about them. Satan, the accuser of the brethren (**Revelation 12:10**), however, will remind you often of those things.

> **Proverbs 23:7** —For as a man thinks in his heart, so is he.

> **Philippians 4:8** — "For the rest, brethren, whatever is true, whatever is worthy of reverence and is honorable and seemly, whatever is just, whatever is pure, whatever is lovely and lovable, whatever is kind and winsome and gracious, if there is any virtue and excellence, if there is anything worthy of praise, think on and weigh and take account of these things [fix your minds on them]" (Amplified Bible).

Satan wants to drop some of the most ungodly thoughts into your mind, just out of the clear blue sky, and them he will immediately say, "I thought you were a Christian." Satan plays dirty, he is not your friend, it was his ugly thought in the first place and then he wants you to feel bad about it. Don't entertain his thoughts, just turn them into something sweet to think on, like how good God is and how wonderful it is to have the written Word of God in our homes, the Old Testament people didn't have that privilege!

Satan wants you to replay the wrongs that have been done to you over and over. That is not productive and it accomplishes nothing good but brings up bitterness and resentment. Forgiveness is very beneficial to your mental health and even to your body. A wise man once said, "Forgiveness is a choice not a feeling." Make the decision to forgive. Talk to the Lord about it and ask Him to help you and He will.

When you practice instantly turning your thoughts to pleasant things, it will become easier and easier and before you know it, those thoughts won't be as much of a problem. We can have victory in our thoughts by making it a habit to adjust and readjust.

> **Psalm 63:4–8** —So will I bless You while I live; I will lift up my hands in Your name. My whole being shall be satisfied as with marrow and fatness; and my mouth shall praise You with joyful lips. When I remember You upon my bed and meditate on You in the night watches. For You have been my help, and in the shadow of Your wings will I rejoice. My whole being follows hard after You and clings closely to You; Your right hand upholds me.

Make it a deliberate thing to praise the Lord and meditate on Him and His promises. It will reinforce, strengthen and grow your faith. Time spent in meditation is well worth it. You think on something all the time anyway because your brain is always running, so why not think about how awesome creation is and how big God is instead of how big your problems are?

> **Psalm 77:11–12** —I will [earnestly] recall the deeds of the Lord; yes, I will [earnestly] remember the wonders [You performed for our fathers] of old. I will meditate also upon all Your works and consider all Your [mighty] deeds (*Amplified Bible*).

I know that all of us have had some times in our lives when God came through for us in an unusual way or at a time when we didn't know how we could have made it through a problem but He did come through.

David had been anointed to be king but wasn't reigning yet because King Saul was still on the throne and in charge. King Saul was jealous when people thought David was a better warrior and pursued David to kill him because he felt his own kingdom was being threatened. That wasn't really true but Saul had allowed his imagination and jealousy to run away with him. David had to go into hiding. David had the opportunity to kill King Saul but he respected Saul too much because of the anointing that God had put on his life.

At another time when David and his men came back to camp after a big battle, they found their town burned and the women and children had been kidnapped. At that time even his own men turned against David, but it says in **1 Samuel 30:6** that David strengthened himself in the Lord his God.

David had lots of problems in his life but God said he was a man after His own heart because he was a worshiper. He wrote a lot of the book of Psalms. (Some of them were written about King Saul chasing him but lots of them were pure worship and thanksgiving for what God had done in his life.) If you don't know how to worship God read the Psalms. When you are going through tough times, pray and worship like King David did. To look back at what God has done in your life is good medicine; remember how He has always answered prayer and always met every need.

In **Matthew 6** there are three times we are advised to not think, worry or be anxious about what we will eat, drink, wear, or even about tomorrow. If there is anything I have learned in my life here on earth is that most of the things I have worried about never happened. The Bible tells us that worry will not change the circumstance but prayer and trust will. God doesn't give us the grace for tomorrow until tomorrow. We only have enough grace for this day. I have learned that there are things that need to be done and things that can wait and by the time I get those things done the day is usually pretty well spent. Don't worry about things, God knows what you need, trust in His provision.

> **Matthew 6:25** —Therefore I say unto you, Take no thought for your life, what you will

eat, or what you will drink; nor about your body, what you will put on. Is not life more than food and the body than clothing?

Matthew 6:34 —Take therefore no thought for the morrow: for tomorrow shall take thought for the things of itself. Sufficient unto the day is the evil thereof.

Abraham in **Romans 4:18–24** believed God. In verse 19 it says: "And being not weak in faith, he considered not his own body now dead, when he was about an hundred years old, neither yet the deadness of Sara's womb." Abraham did not even consider or take any thought about his physical body or that of Sarah's. He didn't spend his time dwelling on the natural body, but spent his time dwelling on God's promise that He would make him the father of many nations. God was true to His Word even when in the natural it looked impossible.

The story found in **Luke 8:41-56** is about Jairus a ruler of the synagogue, who had come to Jesus to heal his daughter. While they were on the way to his house a servant met them and told Jairus that his daughter was dead.

Luke 8:50 —But when Jesus heard it, He answered him, saying, "Fear not: believe only, and she shall be made whole." Or in other words, override the doubt and just believe.

You can have doubt and belief at the same time. We live in a real world. We have senses, (see, hear, smell, taste, and feel). These senses are how we take in and process things in our brain. However, our brain is not saved. Our spirit is saved and it is by the spirit that we believe the things of God. You have probably never seen God but you know that there is a God and His son, Jesus Christ, by the spirit. Even though I have never seen Jesus with my physical eyes, you cannot convince me that He does not exist because I know Him in my spirit.

I am born again in my spirit but I still have a brain that processes things through the natural. It is a computer that runs all the time and it thinks things in the natural. However, through the Word of God we renew our mind and transform our thinking to align and agree with the Word of God. The Word says things that don't make sense to our brain.

For instance: God told the Children of Israel in Joshua 6 to walk around the walls of Jericho for six days without making a sound with their mouths. On the seventh day the priests were to blow their trumpets and have all the people shout and the walls would fall down; but that doesn't make sense to our brain. We would have tried to go through the walls by breaking them down.

In **Judges 7**, God told Gideon to go against the great number of the Midianites and Amalekites with just 300 men. Our brain would have thought we needed more men to outnumber the enemy to win the battle. Your brain cannot take in the things of God but your spirit can by what the Word of God says. That is how we renew our minds.

Let's look at Romans 12:2 again because it fits into this category also and see it with the Greek definitions:

> **Romans 12:2** —"And be not conformed to this world: but be transformed by the renewing of your mind, that you may prove what is that good, and acceptable, and perfect, will of God."
>
> *Transformed*: change or metamorphosis; *renewing*: renovation; and *mind*: intellect, understanding. This means: you are changing and renovating your understanding to agree with the will of God.
>
> This is also found in **Ephesians 4:23**: "And be renewed in the spirit of your mind."

So, can you see that what you say and think really does make a difference in the answered prayers in your life? Let me give an example that will help you further. If someone gave you a huge check, signed and made out to you, and you knew that person had the money in the bank so it could really be cashed upon demand, would you cash it?

What if you wrote **canceled** across the front of that check? When you took it to the bank would they cash it? You could explain to them that the check is good and he has the money and he wants you to have it. They would say, sorry you will have to get another check. So, if you did get another check and you wrote **canceled** across that check also, would the bank be able to cash that check? No!

That is what happens when we try to believe for healing in our bodies but our mouths are talking about the symptoms rather than what the Word of God says about healing. God Himself signed that healing check when Jesus made the Word of God valid for us by appropriating (making it useful and proper) with His blood and His life. Please don't let your words and thoughts write **canceled** on that check.

◄CHAPTER 10►

LAST WALL: DOES GOD LOVE ME?

The afternoon of the day I was healed, Pastor Rick Fern taught the healing school. He spent the whole two hours teaching on how much God loves us. He started in Genesis and went through to Revelation showing me that God loves me. I knew God loved others, and I was just fine with God loving others, but I had a real problem with God loving me.

My earthly dad was unpredictable. He is now in heaven. I love my dad and respect him because he was a hardworking man who took providing for his family very seriously. However I was afraid of Daddy. He was quick-tempered and I never knew what mood he would be in when he came home from work.

Most of the time he was a very happy man. He was self-employed and would sometimes have too much work to do or no work coming in, or the weather hindered him from the work he had to do which stressed him. He also had five kids to support which is a very heavy burden. Dad was never taught mercy and grace. He loved God but he always felt like he fell short; this made life hard for him.

Whatever caused the anger or the stress, as a child growing up it seemed like I had two daddies: the happy one who was so loving, who laughed a lot, sang or whistled or played the French harp, and was easy to talk to, or the angry, hard-to-please Daddy. When he would drive into the driveway of our home I would stop in my tracks and listen. If he was singing or whistling, then all was okay. If I didn't hear one of those then I would watch intently to see the expression on his face when he walked in the door.

If he seem worried or sad, I would try to be very quiet and stay out of his way. Sometimes Dad would be angry and hard to please for days at a time. When he was happy he was very happy and maybe the very things that had made him very angry in the past, would go almost unnoticed by him. That left me very confused.

I became a Christian when I was seven years old. Sometimes I felt like God only loved me because He was somehow obligated to love me. I wanted Him to love me so much but I felt like I always disappointed Him because I wasn't perfect in my walk with Him. I felt unsure of myself even when I would come to Him in prayer. I didn't just bounce into His presence with this huge toothy smile in full assurance of being welcome in His presence. I usually came to talk to Father God with my head down and feeling very unqualified to be there. I would never have had the nerve to call him Daddy God.

I missed out on so much of the loving relationship that God wanted to have with me because of all the confusion with my earthly dad. I never had a clear-cut idea about the rules with Daddy because one time something would make him mad but maybe the next that same thing might not faze him at all. I felt like I was always walking on thin ice and I could break through at any minute. I believe that my loving Heavenly Father sent Rick Fern to teach that day just so I could learn that He really does love us.

I wish I could share all the scriptures that Rick Fern taught that day, but I don't remember the ones he chose. So let me tell you about some of my favorite promises. Of course, I would have to reprint the entire Bible to tell of all the love God has for us. The whole Bible is about God's love for man, and all the blessings, provision, and miracles that He has done on man's behalf...to meet all of man's needs.

My hope is that you will be fully assured that God loves you. It does not matter how you feel about yourself. What matters is what God's Word says about you. I want to show you in scripture some great promises that we have. These are good scriptures to say over your life, over your family, and your friends and neighbors.

Jeremiah 1:5 —Before I formed you in the womb I knew you; and before you were born I sanctified you...

Isaiah 45:2 —"I will go before thee, and make the crooked places straight." This scripture tells us that no matter what road or path that life leads us down, God Himself goes ahead of us to straighten some of those crooked places before we ever come to them and then He will go there with us. How comforting and sweet is that?

Psalm 139:13–18 —For You formed my inward parts; You covered me in my mother's womb. I will praise You, for I am fearfully and wonderfully made; marvelous are Your works, and that my soul knows very well. My frame was not hidden from You, when I was made in secret, and skillfully wrought in the lowest parts of the earth.

Your eyes saw my substance, being yet unformed. And in Your book they all were written, the days fashioned for me, when as yet there were none of them. How precious also are Your thoughts to me, O God! How great is the sum of them! If I should count them, they would be more in number than the sand; when I awake, I am still with You.

These scriptures are such a comfort to me. God has a plan for each one of us. He knew you before you were in the womb, you were not an accident, you were part of His plan.

Psalms 23 and **91** are the places to run to when we need **encouragement**. They are full of the great promises and provision of God for us. Psalms 23 and 91 need to be our 'go to scriptures' when we are afraid. I have included Psalm 91; and I encourage you to keep these scriptures close and read them often when you feel afraid.

Psalm 91:1–16 —He that dwells in the secret place of the Most High shall abide under the shadow of the Almighty. I will say of the LORD, He is my refuge and my fortress: My God, in Him will I trust. Surely He shall deliver you from the snare of the fowler, and from the noisome pestilence.

He shall cover you with His feathers, and under His wings you shall take refuge; His truth shall be your shield and buckler. You shalt not be afraid of the terror by night; nor of the arrow that flies by day; nor of the pestilence that walks in darkness; nor of the destruction that lays waste at noonday.

Because He has set his love upon Me, therefore will I deliver him: I will set him on high, because he has known My name. He shall call upon Me, and I will answer him; I will be with him in trouble, I will deliver him, and honor him. With long life I will satisfy him, and show him My salvation.

Please take the time to do a visual in your mind when reading these two chapters. Use your God-given ability of imagination and see yourself under God's wings of protection. See that in the safety of His feathers we don't have to be afraid. His protection can keep us from having to go through a lot of the things that others have to go through because they don't stay close to God. Oh, that everyone knew how wonderful it is to put their trust in God!

Some people think if they give their life to God they have to give up something. Let's spread the news that the peace and security they receive makes the exchange well worth it; and those things which were not good choices in their past are not missed.

> **Galatians 4:4–7** —But when the fullness of the time had come, God sent forth His Son, born of a woman, born under the law, to redeem those who were under the law, that we might receive the adoption as sons.
>
> And because you are sons, God has sent forth the Spirit of His Son into your hearts, crying out, "Abba, Father!" Therefore you are no longer a slave but a son, and if a son, then an heir of God through Christ.

When I accepted Jesus as my Savior, I was adopted as a son with the full rights of a son and became an heir of God. We are not servants, we are sons.

The story of the prodigal son found in **Luke 15:11–32** is a wonderful story that helps us see the difference between sonship and servanthood and this one also shows the love of a father for his son. Jesus Himself told this story so we know He is talking about Father God. The story is about a man (Father God) who had two sons. The one son came to his dad and asked that his inheritance be given to him right then, rather than waiting until after his father had passed away. That was very presumptuous or like we would say today, "That was a bad deal" to even ask.

The son had all the rights of a son and the father had provided him with everything he needed. He must have thought that he was missing something that the world could offer him. Those thoughts were thoughts that Satan put in there: like "the grass is greener on the other side." But when you get to that other side you see that it only *appeared* greener from a distance. In the Garden of Eden where Adam and Eve lived, God had told them that they could freely eat of every tree, but Satan tempted them by making them think that God was withholding something from them, and they fell for it and that caused the fall of man.

The dad gave his son his inheritance just like the son asked, but the son went far away and spent all the money on riotous living or as we would say "He blew the money"—probably playing the big shot—on things that were, let's just say, ungodly choices. There came a famine in the land. When the son had wasted all his money, he had to get a job feeding pigs! That was a very low position for a Jewish boy to take. Jews were not allowed to eat pork because they were considered unclean. Things got so bad for the boy that he was actually eating the food meant for the pigs. He was eating husks which would have had little if any nutritional value but was just a filler to satisfy the pain of an empty stomach. When you are living like the world and are spiritually away from God, no matter where you go or what you do, there is an emptiness that only the love of God and His peace can fill.

Later, the Bible says that "he came to himself" or in other words it dawned on him one day that he would be much better off to just return home and work for his dad as a hired servant, rather than to die of hunger. His dad had many hired servants and they all had plenty to eat. He probably missed the peace and happiness that was in the father's house.

He probably felt like he was not worthy to be a son and thought the best he could expect was to be treated as a hired servant. Feeling sadness and condemnation, he started home. However, the dad saw him coming from a long way off. He must have been watching for him ever since he left. The Bible says the father ran to him (not from him). He didn't even wait for him to get all the way home but met him before he could get to the father. He fell on the son's neck with a big embrace and kissed him. What a beautiful picture of love and grace even though the son had made the wrong choice by willingly leaving the father.

The son told him I have sinned against heaven and am no longer worthy of being your son. The Bible doesn't say what the father said to the boy, but he didn't have him beaten to teach him a lesson! Instead, he called for the servants and told them to get the best robe (not the worn out one that was all tattered and torn back in the corner somewhere). This is a picture of the robe of righteousness given to us because of the blood of Jesus. It is not because we worked for it or because we had made right choices in our lives but it is the robe of righteousness by the grace of God.

He told them to bring the ring. The ring represented great honor given by the father and was a sign of wealth. The boy had spent all the money the father gave him but the dad restored wealth to him again. This would be like a credit card today, one that he could do business on behalf of his father again just as he did when he was a son with full privileges and responsibilities. The dad told the servant to bring the shoes for the son. It is possible that the servants didn't have shoes but sons do. It showed status, restored relationship, and acceptance from the father. Shoes are protection from the rocks and thorns that lay in the path.

After the dad sent the servant to bring those things, he ran toward the son. The father ran! Doesn't that just bless you to see that picture in your mind? When he got to the son he grabbed him and hugged and kissed him. The dad had also told the servants to kill the fatted calf. If you were not raised on a farm you may not understand what a fatted calf is. You choose a good calf out of the herd and you pen it up separately to feed it good or special grain so that it can fatten up before it is butchered. Then the dad threw this wayward son a big party, a celebration, because his son had finally came home.

Jesus used this story to show the Father's love and forgiveness; and that when you are a son, you are deeply loved and you have privileges and responsibilities that servants don't have. If you struggle with understanding the Father's love because your earthly father didn't love you as he should....you now have a choice to make. You can either believe that Jesus was telling the truth—which He always does, He cannot lie, only Satan lies—or you choose to believe the truth of a loving faithful God who chose you to be the apple of His eye.

Joyce Meyers said that because of the sexual abuse of her earthly father she couldn't trust in her Heavenly Father's love for her. She said she makes a point of looking at herself in the mirror on a regular basis and saying, "God loves me" to herself. She says it over and over. One time she will put the emphasis on *God* and the next time she puts the emphasis on *loves*, and the next on *me*. She says it in different ways out loud until her spirit gets it.

Whatever it takes for you, keep trying to understand this precious, faithful love and kindness that Father God has for you. In some cases it may take a long time, but you will come to believe it. Satan loves it when you have doubt about God's love or provision in any area of your life. Doubt causes us to feel settled and trusting one day and worrying the next. Dig your heels in through the truth of God's Word and see what wonderful promises He has made and make them yours.

I started saying things out loud such as: "God sent me a teacher to my Sunday School Class" and "I know that God sent Pastor Mark to my church so I could learn how to receive my healing." In doing that I was declaring that God personally loves me enough to send people to help me find the way out of that wheelchair. I honestly believe He did that for me. I believe that Rick Fern was led by the Holy Spirit that day when he explained the love of God to us in that class. I had never seen him before and he certainly didn't know me or that I had a problem understanding that God loved me. God did know and I believe he led Brother Fern to the scriptures he shared that day.

> **Deuteronomy 31:8** —And the LORD He is the One who goes before you. He will be with you, He will not fail you, He will not forsake you; do not fear nor be dismayed.

> **Isaiah 41:10** —Fear not, for I am with you: be not dismayed, for I am your God. I will strengthen you. Yes, I will help you, I will uphold you with My righteous right hand.

God is on your side (Ps 118:6). He loves you with an everlasting love. He is not mad at you. He will never leave you or forsake you. When you mess up—and we all do—run *to* God, not *from* him. He will always love you and help you no matter what you have done or how stupid you feel for messing up.

> **Deuteronomy 7:9** —Know therefore that the LORD your God, He is God, the faithful God, which keeps the covenant and mercy with them that love Him and keep His commandments to a thousand generations.

You may think, "I have never done anything right in my life," or, "I have never made a difference in anyone's life." But in this scripture it says if you have made the decision to follow God, that means your children and their descendants will be blessed for a thousand generations. There is nothing greater than having God's blessings on our children. He is with them when we cannot be with them. We can't live for a thousand generations, so it is comforting to know that He will still be blessing our grandchildren and their children's children long after we are in heaven with Him.

> **Ephesians 2:4** —But God, who is rich in mercy, for His great love wherewith He loved us." Rich in the Greek means wealthy, figuratively it means abounding with.

> **Isaiah 54:13–14** —All your children shall be taught of the LORD; and great shall be the peace of your children. (We all want our children to have great peace. This is a wonderful promise of the LORD.) In righteousness you shall be established: you shall be far from oppression; for you shall not fear: and from terror; for it shall not come near you.

> **Jeremiah 31:3** —The LORD has appeared of old unto me, saying, Yes, I have loved you with an everlasting love: therefore with loving kindness I have drawn you.

> **Romans 8:35–39** —Who shall separate us from the love of Christ? Shall tribulation, or

distress, or persecution, or famine, or nakedness, or peril, or sword? For I am persuaded that neither death nor life, nor angels nor principalities nor powers, nor things present nor things to come, nor height nor depth, nor any other created thing, shall be able to separate us from the love of God which is in Christ Jesus our Lord.

It seems like in our fast paced lives that even sleep is a rare commodity, but like everything else we need, there are promises for that also in the Bible.

Proverbs 3:24 —When you lie down, you shall not be afraid; yes, you shall lie down, and your sleep shall be sweet.

Psalm 3:5 —I laid me down and slept; I awaked; for the LORD sustained me.

Psalm 4:8 —I will both lay me down in peace, and sleep: for you, LORD, only make me dwell in safety.

I know me all too well, and I know my shortcomings. I had always felt like I had let God down, that He was mad at me because I wasn't perfect. I really needed to hear that God loves me. Maybe you need to hear that, too.

Knowing that God loved me was my last obstacle, the last wall, that stood between me and receiving my healing and now I was ready to be prayed for.

◀CHAPTER 11▶

THE NIGHT I WAS HEALED

By the time of the healing school, the RSD was in both legs from my hips down and in both feet. My hands and arms were involved because of the wheelchair and I wore braces on them to sleep and sometimes in the daytime. After about three weeks of the healing school and finding out what the Word really says and renewing my mind with the Word and getting my spirit in line with the Word, I went down to the prayer line to have hands laid on me for prayer to receive my healing.

That night Brother Rick Fern was praying for the sick and said, "Don't look to me for your healing because I'm not the healer, Jesus is your healer. Close your eyes and see Jesus, He is the healer." So I closed my eyes and I saw in my mind that picture we've all seen where the artist shows Jesus holding out His hands.

When Rick Fern and Pastor Mark got to where I was praying, they prayed for me, and then went on. I, of course, kept praying and in a couple of minutes I started crying and crying. It had been a long thirteen years and it had been so hard. But then after a while I began to laugh and laugh. The whole time I was trying to tell myself to not be loud, but I wanted to be loud.

Then the laughter stopped and I sat on the front pew for a minute and I had this wonderful urge to run around the inside of the sanctuary. The sanctuary is a big place and it's on an incline which had made it hard for me in the past. When I came down for prayer, there was no way I could have gone that far but, I started walking. I wanted to run but I thought I needed to calm down, so I walked completely around the room. I was gloriously healed! I wanted to scream, "**I Am So Healed!**"

That night, when I got home, I told my husband that I was healed and he started crying too. I told my daughters and we were all so happy, but they were afraid to believe it. As the days went on I was doing things that I had not done in years. Walking, running, getting down on the floor with my grandkids to play and I was even riding on the back of a four wheeler with one of my grandsons. I was cleaning house and busy again.

On the outsides of my legs by my shin bones I had a visible disfigurement like big pones all the way from my knees to my ankles and in three days that was completely gone. That is when my family really started getting it. That was in August 2004.

However that is not the end of my testimony, remember how the whole thing started with a little annoying throb under my right ankle? Well that throb started again, just days after my healing. **John**

10:10 says "the thief comes to steal and to kill and to destroy." Satan was trying to steal my healing. I had read a book a few years before called *There is a Miracle in Your Mouth* by John Olsteen, so I was **careful** not to **say** anything about it to anyone. The Bible says we have power in our tongues.

Satan was telling me that I wasn't healed and that somehow I was in some "strange remission," and the RSD was starting all over again. But this time I was armed with the Word. The Bible says that Satan is a liar and the father of all lies. As someone said, "If his lips are moving he is lying!" I was not going to believe his lies. So I kept praising God. I really was healed in my hands, arms, legs and feet, I was not in all that awful pain, but it was just that little throb.

We have a circle in our home where you can go from room to room and end up back where you started and so I'd just walk the circle preaching to Satan all the time: "Satan, you're a liar! Jesus took my infirmities, bore my sickness. He healed my diseases and by His stripes I was healed." Then I'd say **Psalm 103**, "Bless the Lord O my soul, and all that is within me bless His holy name. Bless the Lord O my soul and forget not all His benefits, who forgives all my iniquities and heals all my diseases."

When Satan came against Jesus in the wilderness to tempt him Jesus always said, "It is written," and He would quote the Old Testament to him, but we have a new and better covenant, the New Testament.

That throb went on for a long, long time, but I just kept standing on the Word and praising God. Then I read a book by Kenneth Hagin about **Mark 11:23**, where he talked about speaking to the mountain. So I started speaking to my ankle telling it to line up with the Word and be whole and in a couple of weeks the throbbing stopped. I am convinced had I not stood on the Word that I would have lost my healing!

Several years after I was healed, Jerry and I were watching a television show. There was a panel of doctors talking about the pain of RSD. They said that some patients with RSD are committed to insane asylums because they cannot stand the pain. I wasn't a weakling, but there were times that I just wanted to start screaming. I remember being afraid that if I ever started, I wouldn't be able to stop.

I was sick and in pain for thirteen years, in a wheelchair, and tormented by the insurance company who tried every way they knew how to prove that I was faking my illness...**but God**! Don't you just love those two words together? The Bible is full of 'But Gods' and I know you have some "But God's" in your life where the Lord came through for you.

Multitudes came to Jesus **but Jesus** always healed them all of every disease and sickness. The Bible is full of people who dared to believe God for something and whatever they believed for is what they got. The Lord is looking for believers. The word *believe* is in the Bible 143 times. Jesus says *believe* in the book of John 35 times.

Why don't you dare to believe God today?

> In **Luke 5:12** (remember, Luke was a physician) it says: And it happened when He was in a certain city, that behold, a man who was full of leprosy saw Jesus; and he fell on his face and implored Him, saying, "Lord, if You are willing, You can make me clean." Then He put out His hand and touched him, saying, "**I am willing**; be cleansed." Immediately the leprosy left him.

There is a saying that says, "Faith is not believing that God can, but *knowing* He will. I'd like to take that a little further and say, "Faith is not believing that God can, but knowing He will for you today!!!

◀CHAPTER 12▶

HEALING SCRIPTURES

There are lots of scriptures in the Old and New Testaments about healing. This will not be a complete list. The first three I have here are my favorite ones. There is no way that I can close this book without sharing these three most powerful healing scriptures. I quote the complete scripture, from the King James Bible then I restate the same scripture after studying them in the Greek or Hebrew translations. The insight of the original translations really state the full meaning of most of the words. I hope you find these to be the nuggets you need to see that healing is for today.

The purpose of the Greek translations is to put each word under the microscope of the complete meaning. This amplifies the scripture so there is no doubt what they are saying. These are key, powerful weapons of our warfare to put front and center of our arsenal. I have also left blanks for you to fill your name in to make it personally about you.

Luke 10:19 —Behold, I give unto you power to tread on serpents and scorpions, and over all the power of the enemy: and nothing shall by any means hurt you.

After inserting the Greek meanings of the words this same scripture can be read like this: See, I (Jesus), grant (put your name here), super human authority and the right and strength, to trample under your feet, Satan, and over all the power of the Satan, or any foe, and nothing (nobody or anything at all) shall in any means or way, harm you physically or injure (put your name here).

Satan doesn't want you to know that this scripture exists much less put it in the front of your arsenal against him!

Isaiah 54:17 —No weapon that is formed against you shall prosper; and every tongue that shall rise against you in judgment *you shall condemn*. This is the heritage of the servants of the Lord, and their righteousness is of me, says the Lord.

This scripture with the Hebrew insight can be read like this: No weapon, gun, or tool whatsoever, that is made for any purpose against (put your name here), will be able to come or go over (put your name here), and anyone whatsoever, that says anything evil against (put your name here), any words spoken over (put your name here) that try to rear up against (put your name here), in any unfavorable sentence, such as a bad diagnosis, or anything that would try to make trouble for (put your name here), I (Put your name here in capital letters!) will declare wrong!

I was declared permanently and totally disabled by a judge in a court of law. All of those doctors said I would have to take pain medication for the rest of my life. When we get a bad report from the doctor, we don't have to accept it. *I set before you this day life and death. Choose therefore life* (**Deuteronomy 30:14–19**). According to God's Word, we have choices. See what the Word says and come into agreement with what God says. God is higher than any doctor or doctor's report.

The last part of that scripture says *you shall condemn* (you have to declare it wrong). Don't receive the bad report. Don't look at how big your mountain is, look at how big your God is.

> The rest of **Isaiah 54:17** can be read like this: This is our possession, given to us by God, and (put your name here) am a bondservant, those who choose to follow Him because we love Him and by free choice serve him, Jehovah God, Abba Father, daddy God and (put your name here), righteousness and right standing is because my God, Himself, declared me righteous.

> **Matthew 8:17b** —Himself took our infirmities, and bore our sicknesses.

This one with the Greek definitions could be read like this: Jesus, Himself, took (past tense) from us, (put your name here), sicknesses, disease, weakness, and feebleness, and He removed them, lifted and took them up. In this scripture Jesus was quoting Isaiah 53 about His own beating and death.

Isaiah 53:5 —But He was wounded for our transgressions, He was bruised for our iniquities: the chastisement of our peace was upon Him; and with His stripes we are healed.

These are more Old Testament healing scriptures. I like to underline scriptures that are special to me so they are easily found. This list of healing scriptures was compiled in part by my sister, Juanita Hascall. I have used this list many times.

Exodus 23:25 —So you shall serve the Lord your God, and He will bless your bread and your water. And I will take sickness away from the midst of you.

Deuteronomy 7:15a —And the Lord will take away from you all sickness, and will afflict you with none of the terrible diseases of Egypt which you have known...

Deuteronomy 34:7 —And Moses was an hundred and twenty years old when he died: his eye was not dim, nor his natural force abated.

Psalm 30:2 —O Lord my God, I cried out to You and You healed me.

Psalm 41:3 — The Lord will strengthen him on his bed of illness; You will sustain him on his sickbed.

Psalm 91:10 — No evil shall befall you, nor shall any plague come near your dwelling.

Psalm 91:11 —For He shall give His angels charge over you, to keep you in all your ways.

Psalm 91:14 — Because he has set his love upon Me, therefore I will deliver him; I will set him on high, because he has known My name.

Psalm 91:15 —He shall call upon me, and I will answer him: I will be with him in trouble; I will deliver him, and honor him.

Psalm 91:16 —With long life will I satisfy him, and shew him my salvation.

Psalm 103:2 —Bless the Lord, O my soul, and forget not all His benefits:

Psalm 103:3 —Who forgives all your iniquities, who heals all your diseases.

Psalm 103:4 —Who redeems your life from destruction; who crowns thee with loving-kindness and tender mercies;

Psalm 103:5 —Who satisfies your mouth with good things; so that your youth is renewed like the eagle's.

Psalm 107:19 —Then they cry unto the LORD in their trouble, and He saves them out of their distresses.

Psalm 107:20 —He sent His word, and healed them, and delivered them from their destructions. (This scripture is referenced to **Matt 8:8** —"The centurion answered and said, Lord, I am not worthy that You should come under my roof: but speak the word only, and my servant shall be healed.")

Isaiah 58:11 —The Lord will guide you continually, and satisfy your soul in drought, and strengthen your bones; you shall be like a watered garden, and like a spring of water, whose waters do not fail.

Isaiah 66:13 —As one whom his mother comforts, so will I comfort you; and you shall be comforted in Jerusalem.

Isaiah 66:14 —And when you see this, your heart shall rejoice, and your bones shall flourish like an herb: and the hand of the Lord shall be known toward His servants, and his indignation toward His enemies.

Jeremiah 30:17a —For I will restore health unto you, and I will heal you of your wounds, says the LORD.

My prayer is that you can clearly see that there are healing scriptures in both the Old and New Testaments and that healing is God's heart for His people and that you can still be healed today because God does not change.

THE NEW TESTAMENT HEALING SCRIPTURES:

Matthew, Mark, Luke and John are the books that talk about Jesus' ministry on earth and a big part of that ministry was healing. As I suggested earlier in this book, when you read the Gospels underline all the healings and circle where it says *all* and *every* so you can clearly see Jesus as the healer to everyone. I will, however, list a few healing scriptures from the New Testament because I want to point out that Jesus was not the only one who had a healing ministry.

I have heard people say that only Jesus or some say Jesus and the apostles (disciples) were the only ones in the New Testament who had a healing ministry. In the following scriptures, Jesus, the twelve, the seventy, and also Stephen, Philip, and Paul had healing ministries (even after Jesus went to heaven). Then we see Paul teaching how the gifts of the spirit are to be used in the church; he also taught that there would be healing, and miracles. Jesus instructed all the believers who followed him to heal the sick. In the Great Commission Jesus said that healings and miracles will be the signs of a believer. Christians are the believers

THE DISCIPLES:

Matt 10:1 —And when He had called unto Him His twelve disciples, He gave them power against unclean spirits, to cast them out, and to heal all manner of sickness and all manner of disease.

Matt 10:2 —Now the names of the twelve apostles are these; The first, Simon, who is called Peter, and Andrew his brother; James the son of Zebedee, and John his brother;

Matt 10:3 —Philip and Bartholomew; Thomas, and Matthew the publican; James the son of Alphaeus, and Lebbaeus, whose surname was Thaddaeus;

Matt 10:5-6 —These twelve Jesus sent forth, and commanded them, saying, Go not into the way of the Gentiles, and into any city of the Samaritans enter not: (we covered in an earlier chapter that Jesus came to the Jews first then to the Gentiles.) But go rather to the lost sheep of the house of Israel.

Matt 10:7-8 —And as you go, preach, saying, The kingdom of heaven is at hand. Heal the sick, cleanse the lepers, raise the dead, cast out devils: freely you have received, freely give.

The above scriptures clearly explain that Jesus gave the disciples power to heal all sickness and disease. These next few verses (not listed here) explain the directions Jesus gave. Notice verse 8. It clearly states that the disciples were to heal the sick.

The disciples still had a healing ministry after Jesus ascended to heaven:

> **Acts 3:2–5** — And a certain man lame from his mother's womb was carried, whom they laid daily at the gate of the temple which is called Beautiful, to ask alms from those who entered the temple; who, seeing Peter and John about to go into the temple, asked for alms. And fixing his eyes on him, with John, Peter said, "Look at us." So he gave them his attention, expecting to receive something from them.

> **Act 3:6–8** — Then Peter said, "Silver and gold I do not have, but what I do have I give you: In the name of Jesus Christ of Nazareth, rise up and walk." And he took him by the right hand and lifted him up, and immediately his feet and ankle bones received strength. So he, leaping up, stood and walked and entered the temple with them—walking, leaping, and praising God. And all the people saw him walking and praising God.

THE SEVENTY

Luke 10:1 — After these things the Lord appointed seventy others also, and sent them two by two before His face into every city and place where He Himself was about to go. (In verses 2–8 Jesus taught them what to do when they entered a city. You can read that for yourself.)

Luke 10:9 —And heal the sick that are therein, and say unto them, The kingdom of God is come near to you. (This verse clearly shows that the seventy were to heal the sick.)

STEPHEN

After Jesus rose from the dead and went to heaven the twelve disciples chose seven men to serve in some of the business that needed tending so they could spend more time in the Word. Verse 8 tells us that Stephen did great wonders and miracles. He was not with Jesus, and was not one of the twelve or seventy that Jesus appointed because the disciples chose both Stephen and Philip.

Acts 6:2–3 —Then the twelve called the multitude of the disciples unto them, and said, it is not desirable that we should leave the Word of God, and serve tables. Wherefore, brethren, look ye out among you seven men of honest report, full of the Holy Ghost and wisdom, whom we may appoint over this business.

Acts 6:4–5 —But we will give ourselves continually to prayer, and to the ministry of the word. And the saying pleased the whole multitude: and they chose Stephen, a man full of faith and of the Holy Ghost, and Philip, and Prochorus, and Nicanor, and Timon, and Parmenas, and Nicolas a proselyte of Antioch:

Act 6:8 —And Stephen, full of faith and power, did great wonders and miracles among the people.

PHILIP

Acts 8:5–7 —Then Philip went down to the city of Samaria, and preached Christ unto them. And the people with one accord gave heed unto those things which Philip spoke, hearing and seeing the miracles which he did. For unclean spirits, crying with loud voice, came out of many that were possessed with them: and many taken with palsies, and that were lame, were healed.

PAUL

Acts 14:8–11 —And there sat a certain man at Lystra, impotent in his feet, being a cripple from his mother's womb, who never had walked. The same heard Paul speak: who steadfastly beholding him, and perceiving that he had faith to be healed said with a loud voice, "Stand upright on thy feet!" And he leaped and walked. And when the people saw what Paul had done, they lifted up their voices, saying in the speech of Lycaonia, "The gods are come down to us in the likeness of men."

Act 19:11–12—And God wrought special miracles by the hands of Paul: so that from his body were brought unto the sick handkerchiefs or aprons, and the diseases departed from them, and the evil spirits went out of them.

Paul taught the gifts of the spirit to the Corinthians and how they are to work in the church body. Look at verses 9 and10.

1 Corinthians 12:4–5 —Now there are distinctive varieties and distributions of endowments (gifts, extraordinary powers distinguishing certain Christians, due to the power of divine grace operating in their souls by the Holy Spirit) and they vary, but the [Holy] Spirit remains the same. And there are distinctive varieties of service and ministration, but it is the same Lord [Who is served].

1 Corinthians 12:9–10 —To another [wonder-working] faith by the same [Holy] Spirit, to another the extraordinary powers of healing by the one Spirit; to another the working of miracles, to another prophetic insight (the gift of interpreting the divine will and purpose); to another the ability to discern and distinguish between [the utterances of true] spirits [and false ones], to another various kinds of [unknown] tongues, to another the ability to interpret [such] tongues.

1 Corinthians 12:11–12 —All these [gifts, achievements, abilities] are inspired and brought to pass by one and the same [Holy] Spirit, Who apportions to each person individually [exactly] as He chooses. For just as the body is a unity and yet has many parts, and all the parts, though many, form [only] one body, so it is with Christ (the Messiah, the Anointed One).

2 Corinthians 12:13 —For by [means of the personal agency of] one [Holy] Spirit we were all, whether Jews or Greeks, slaves or free, baptized [and by baptism united together] into one body, and all made to drink of one [Holy] Spirit.

Further instructions from James to believers: These scriptures were also used previously in this book.

James 5:14–15 —Is any sick among you? Let him call for the elders of the church; and let them pray over him, anointing him with oil in the name of the Lord: And the prayer of faith shall save the sick, and the Lord shall raise him up; and if he have committed sins, they shall be forgiven him.

James 5:16 —Confess your faults one to another, and pray one for another, that you may be healed. The effectual fervent prayer of a righteous man avails much.

The Great Commission, the last instructions that Jesus gave to all believers before He left for heaven:

Mark 16:15–16 —And He said unto them, Go into all the world, and preach the gospel to every creature. He that believes and is baptized shall be saved; but he that believes not shall be damned.

Mark 16:17–19 —And these signs shall follow them that believe; in My name shall they cast out devils; they shall speak with new tongues; they shall take up serpents; and if they drink any deadly thing, it shall not hurt them; they shall lay hands on the sick, and they shall recover. So then after the Lord had spoken unto them, He was received up into heaven, and sat on the right hand of God.

It is Jesus' will for the healing ministry to go on through believers now. If we *believe* we should be doing the same works Jesus did in his earthly ministry; and a large part of His ministry was healing the sick.

John 14:12 —Verily, verily, I say unto you, He that believes on me, the works that I do shall he do also; and greater works than these shall he do; because I go unto my Father.

◄CHAPTER 13►

KINGDOM TAKEN BY FORCE

Earlier we talked about the woman of Canaan who asked Jesus to heal her daughter. She didn't let timing stand in her way of being healed. But, that is not the only obstacle she faced. Jesus didn't even answer her and the disciples must have seemed hard-hearted to her need. They even asked Jesus to send her away because she was crying after them for help.

In that day and age, women were not revered. But she didn't let silence from Jesus, or the lack of compassion from the disciples or the tradition of the times stand in the way! She could have become discouraged and quit trying. She had heard about Jesus' healing ministry, she believed in Him and she wanted healing for her daughter more than anything.

There is another woman in the New Testament who was determined to receive healing for herself. The story is found in **Luke 8:43–48**. This woman had been hemorrhaging for twelve years. She had heard of Jesus and said, *If I just touch the hem of his garment, I will be made whole.* There are some things that show just how determined she was to be healed. 1) Surely, after bleeding for twelve years she had to be weak. But she pushed her way through a crowd to touch Jesus' clothes. 2) In that society a person was considered unclean if they were bleeding and according to Mosaic Law you were not supposed to be around other people. She went anyway regardless of those obstacles and was healed.

> **Matthew 11:12** —And from the days of John the Baptist until now the kingdom of heaven suffers violence, and the violent take it by force.

The Greek definition of *violence* and *violent* is seized. I looked up the Greek meaning of *seized* and it said: to fasten upon, be strong, (courageous) to bind, restrain, conquer, be established, be stout, wax strong or stronger, take (hold), be urgent, or withstand.

> This scripture could be read as: And from the days of John the Baptist until right now the kingdom realm, of heaven, or the gospel of Christianity is seized by the violent, the one who will force it energetically, who will take it, or who seizes it by force, and those who are strong and courageous enough to bind and restrain the problem until it is conquered.

Establish these things: "**I will not be denied anything that Jesus has established for me!!** Be urgent, not passive. Take the words "Oh well" and

"I can't help that" out of your vocabulary. Jesus did it all; He is everything that we need. He died for us. Line up your spirit with what He has already done. It is yours, take it!

> **1 Timothy 6:12** —Fight the good fight of faith, lay hold on eternal life, whereunto thou art also called, and hast professed a good profession before many witnesses.

Fight here means: endeavor to accomplish something, fervently declaring the Word of God and his promises over our circumstances. Satan did not catch me by surprise when he tried to steal my healing. I had to fight him with the Word of God and I remained tenacious in that battle.

Don't lose your focus. Satan wants to steal your thought life. He wants your mind on the problem, not what the Word of God has said about your problem, and certainly not on praising God and resting in how Jesus has already solved your problems. Satan has many, many smoke screens, problems, lack of money, fear, pain, sickness, and disease; you name it and he's got it.

> **John 16:33** —In the world you will have tribulation: but be of good cheer; I have overcome the world.

> **2 Peter 1:3** —According as His divine power has given unto us all things that pertain unto life and godliness, through the knowledge of Him that has called us to glory and virtue.

He has given (past tense) unto us, (that's you and me, in the here and now), all things that pertain unto life and godliness, (how?) through the knowledge of Him. The knowledge found in His Word.

> **Mark 13:10–11** —And the gospel must first be published among all nations. But when they shall lead you, and deliver you up, take no thought beforehand what you shall speak, neither do you premeditate: but whatsoever shall be given you in that hour that speak: for it is not you that speaks, but the Holy Ghost.

Verse 11 says take *no thought beforehand* (the Greek means to *care anxiously in advance*); neither do you *premeditate* (the Greek means to *revolve in the mind, imagine*).

These scriptures were talking about Christians being taken to court for their belief in the Gospel. I used these scriptures when I was taken to court by the insurance company who tried over and over to prove I didn't have Reflex Sympathetic Dystrophy. They didn't want to take financial responsibility for the doctors and medication of a condition that is permanent and has no cure.

I was taking two kinds of morphine and one of them cost more than $1,000 a month not to mention all the other medications that I had to take. It was so hard to get my mind to be quiet! What if they made the court believe that I didn't have RSD? How could we ever afford the medication? We couldn't pay more than $1,000 a month. I was in so much pain with the medicine, how could I make it without the medication?

But God had a better plan. Jesus had already took the stripes for my healing! Once I received that healing I didn't need the money, because I didn't have to take all that medication. I didn't have to be in fear of the insurance company or the court or more doctors or more bad reports. Jesus has already paid it all! **It is finished forevermore!**

> **Colossians 2:15** —And having spoiled principalities and powers, He made a shew of them openly, triumphing over them.

> **2 Corinthians 10:3–5** —For though we walk in the flesh, we do not war according to the flesh. For the weapons of our warfare are not carnal but mighty in God for pulling down strongholds, casting down arguments and every high thing that exalts itself against the knowledge of God, bringing every thought into captivity to the obedience of Christ.

Cast down those worries, fears and the torments of Satan that try to be bigger than the knowledge of God's Word.

> **2 Timothy 1:7** —For God has not given us the spirit of fear; but of power, and of love, and of a sound mind.

I had to *take* my healing, it didn't just fall on me because Pastor Mark understood the Word of God about healing, I had to know what the Word says about the healing. It wasn't because of his faith, it was my faith! It is a battle; but it is a battle that is already won. We know the outcome of this battle.

The Word says He teaches **us** to make war. He makes **us** strong.

> **2 Samuel 22:35** —He teaches my hands to make war, so that my arms can bend a bow of bronze.

> **Psalm 18:34** —He teaches my hands to make war, So that my arms can bend a bow of bronze.

> **Psalm 144:1** —Blessed be the Lord my Rock, Who trains my hands for war, and my fingers for battle.

Getting ready to go to the healing school, driving there, loading and unloading that wheel chair day after day was not easy. My normal pain which I could barely stand was so much worse but I had to do whatever it took to get there so I could be taught the truth of God's Word.

Even after my healing I had to fight Satan with the Word and I had to be unmovable in my mind and in the belief of the Word to keep my healing. Keeping my healing was not fighting my mind and Satan just one time. I resisted his lies every day for months. I did not give up and say, "Well it didn't work for me."

I had to take charge of my life with the Word of God, which is the only way to have victory over Satan.

And, believe me when I say he didn't give up easily either. But, I was settled in the knowledge of the Word, which makes it hard to be moved.

Get God's promises forever settled; know that they are yours and no demon in hell or Satan himself can move you because you have God's Word on it!

◀CHAPTER 14▶

SUPER SAINT?

Before I close this book, I want to make completely sure you understand that I am not a super saint. I have not cornered the market on faith. It is not about my faith, it is about His faithfulness. This book is not about me. It is about a loving God who made provision for my healing long before I needed to be healed, but I didn't understand that.

The enemy that kept me in a wheel chair and in pain was "my lack of knowledge," and not knowing the love of my God and His provision that had already been made for me by my wonderful Abba Father. I knew I didn't love Him perfectly, because I am human. But, I didn't understand that He loves me perfectly because Jesus was perfection for me.

Once I understood the Word and the love of the Father, I was healed. I have been healed for ten years (at the time of this writing) and I do have that happy, busy, abundant life that the Lord wants me to have.

I am still amazed at being healed. When I run to the mailbox or get on a horse or ride with my family on a four-wheeler or even when I am able to help someone else for a change, I am thrilled! I smile at Father and thank Him for His goodness and mercy.

While writing this book I can't help but reflect on what my family and I went through those thirteen years and see the contrast of the pain-free wonderful life I have now. My heart shudders to even think where I would be now all these years later if I had not been healed. At the time of this writing, this progressive disease would have been ten years worse. Would I have been on even more pain medications by now? Would the pain have increased so by now that I would be deemed insane and put in an institution? My sister and I used to sing my grandpa's favorite song as a special in church "Where Could I Go Without the Lord?" Now I could sing it as "Where Would I Be Without the Lord?"

In **Joel 2:25** the Lord says He will *restore what the devourer has stolen*. I am not just restored to a life with no pain, but my whole family's lives have been restored. My prayer is that I am anointed to see you restored back to health through this book, by teaching one on one, or by telling my testimony in churches, small groups or meetings.

I don't believe for one moment that God put RSD on me so I would have a ministry. Now that I know how God loves me and how He is a God of abundance, I know that when He restores He gives back much more than what you lost and then anoints you to help others who have gone through similar things.

When you believe God for great and mighty things you will have great and mighty things and you can show the way through your victories to others. What a deal!

###

About the Author

Marquetta Killgore is married to her best friend and the love of her life, Jerry. They have two grown daughters and four beautiful grandchildren. Marquetta's passion and heart is to tell others about the miracle healing God did in her body and that He will heal every one of every disease. She hopes to teach a healing school someday soon. She says, "Almost everything I do on a daily basis is a miracle. I can run to the mailbox which is just at the end of my drive. Before I had to drive there. At church I now can stand, pat my foot, clap my hands and even sway to the music while worshiping the Lord. I could not do any of that before. I couldn't wear high heels or even cross my legs while sitting."

This is Marquetta's personal testimony and can be proven with medical records. Jerry has estimated that the diagnosis was confirmed by at least sixteen doctors. Today Marquetta has traveled in the State of Oklahoma telling the good news that God does heal today, it is His will to heal, and He will heal you, too. People have been healed after hearing her testimony, even some who did not believe in healing at all beforehand. She is available to speak to your group or church.

Marquetta and Jerry live on the farm where Jerry was raised. Marquetta loves to garden and together they usually grow a vegetable garden. Jerry keeps the lawn looking pretty and Marquetta works in the flower beds. Together they make the place look nice.

Marquetta and Jerry are both retired and live in Tecumseh, Oklahoma.

Connect with Marquetta Killgore

I really appreciate you reading my book! Here are my social media coordinates:

Like my Page on Facebook: https://www.facebook.com/pages/Marquetta-Killgore/594102054024176

Favorite my Smashwords author page: https://www.smashwords.com/profile/view/MarquettaKillgore

Send me an email at: marq1124@gmail.com